WOMEN OF LETTERS
An AMS Reprint Series

MEMOIRS
OF THE
LIFE
OF
Mrs. *MANLEY*

AMS PRESS
NEW YORK

F. LaPergne del.   M.V.d. Gucht Sc.

MEMOIRS
OF THE
LIFE
OF
Mrs. *MANLEY*.

(Author of the *Atalantis*.)

CONTAINING

Not only the History of Her Adventures, but likewise an Account of the most considerable Amours in the Court of King Charles the IId.

The Gods of Love *and* Wit *inspire her Pen,*
And Love *and* Beauty *is her constant Theme.*
                                        Mrs. Behn.

To which is added, A Compleat Key.

The Third Edition.

LONDON:
Printed for E. Curll, at the *Dial* and *Bible* against St. *Dunstan's* Church in *Fleetstreet.* 1717.

Price 1 s. 6 d. Stitch'd, 2 s. Bound in Sheep, 2 s. 6 d. in Calves Leather.

Library of Congress Cataloging in Publication Data

Manley, Mary de La Rivière, 1663-1724.
   Memoirs of the life of Mrs. Manley, author of the
Atalantis.

   (Women of letters)
   First published in 1714 under title: The adventures
of Rivella.
   Reprint of the 1717 ed. printed for E. Curll, London.
PR3545.M8A65   1976   823'.5   71-37701
ISBN 0-404-56765-7

Reprinted from an original copy in the collections
of the University of Chicago Library

From the edition of 1717, London
First AMS edition published in 1976
Manufactured in the United States of America

AMS PRESS INC.
NEW YORK, N. Y. 10003

THE

TRANSLATOR's

PREFACE.

THE French *Publisher* has told his Reader, that ' the Means by ' which he became Master of
' the

' *the following* Papers, *was*
' *by his being* Gentleman of
' the Chamber *to the Young*
' Chevalier D'Aumont *when*
' *he was in* England *with the*
' *Ambassador of that Name.* He
' *recounts in his* Preface,*that af-*
' *ter the Conference in* Somer-
' set-house Garden, *those two*
' *Persons were at Supper toge-*
' *ther, where himself attended;*
' *and that the Young* Cheva-
' lier *laid a* Discretion *with*
' *Sir* Charles Lovemore *(who*
' *reproach'd him with not be-*
' *ing attentive to his Relation)*
' *that he would recite to him*
' *upon Paper most of what he*
' *had discours'd with him that*
'   *Even-*

' *Evening, as a Proof both of the Goodness of his Memory, and great Attention: That soon after he, the Publisher, was employ'd at several Times, as* Amanuensis *to the said* Chevalier, *by which Means the Papers remain'd in his Hands at the Death of young* D'Aumont, *which happen'd by a Fever, soon after his Return into* France.'

The English *Reader is desir'd to take Notice that the Verses are not to be found in the* French *Copy; but to make the Book more perfect, Care has been taken to transcribe them*

with

with great *Exactness from the* English *printed* Tragedy *of the same* Author, *yet extant among us.*

London, June 3d, 1714.

THE

A KEY to the Adventures of *RIVELLA*.

RIVELLA,	Author of the *Atalantis*.
Sir *Charles Lovemore*,	Lieuten. Gen. *Tidcomb*.

Pag.

5 Mr. *C*.	Mr. *C——t*, Son to the Lord *B——re*.
13 Mr. *S---le*,	Mr. *Steele*.
19 *Lysander*,	Mr. *Carlisle*.
30 *Hilaria*,	Late D———ſs of *Cleveland*.
31 A Lady next Door to the poor Recluse,	Nominal Mrs. *Rider*, Sir *Richard Fanshaw*'s Daughter, Sister to Mrs. *Blount*, Housekeeper to the Lord *S—rs*.
33 Count *Fortunatus*,	D— of *M———gh*.
—— Kitchin-Maid married to her Master,	Pretended Madam *Beauclair*.
34 Her Patroness's Eldest Son,	Duke of *C—nd* and *S—ton*.
—— Young Lady of little or no Fortune,	Late Lady *Poultney*'s Daughter, D———ſs *Ditto*.
35 The Man *Hilaria* was in Love with,	Mr. *Goodman*, the Player.
—— He kept a Mistress in the next Street,	Mrs. *Wilson*, of the Pope's-Head Tavern in *Cornhill*.
37 The First Dutchess in *England*,	Late Dutchess of *Norfolk*.
45 Sir *Peter Vainlove*,	Sir *Thomas Skipwith*.
48 Mrs. *Settee*,	Mrs. *P—m*.

Pag.
53 Lord *Crafty*,
57 Merchant *Double*,   Late D— of A—*marle*.
—— Baron *Meanwell*,   Late E—l of B—*h*.
59 Old *Double*,   General *Monk*.
—— Two Prelates of the   The Two Peers.
    Church of *England*,
60 Bought the Merchant's   The Two Mrs. *Wrights*, in
    Widow of her Two   *Bloomsbury-Square*.
    Women,
61 *Tim. Double*,   *Christopher Monk*, Son to Colonel *Monk*.
62 *Petty-pan* Merchant,   Mr. *Hungerford*, a Pastry-Cook in *Limestreet*.
64 *Calista*,   Mrs. *Trotter*, a Poetess.
—— *Cleander*,   Mr. *Tilly*.
—— *Oswald*,   The late *John Manley*, Esq; Member of Parliament, and Surveyor-General.
79 The Chief Seat of the   *New-Hall*, in *Essex*.
    Doubles,
86 *Bella*,   *Kitty Baker*, an Actress.
87 *Flippanta*,   Servant to *Rivella*.
92 Old *Simon*,   Mr. *Simson*, Retainer to the Family.
105 A Rich Young Widow,   Mr. *Geo. Smith*'s Widow of *Doctors-Commons*, now Mrs. *Tilly*.
113 Secretary, who examin'd   *John Hopkins*, Esq;
    Rivella,
118 The Person, who publickly and gravely   *Richard Steele*, Esq;
    ask'd *Rivella*'s Pardon,

F I N I S.

THE
HISTORY
OF
RIVELLA.

✤✤✤✤✤✤✤✤✤✤✤✤✤✤✤✤✤✤✤✤✤✤✤✤✤✤✤✤✤✤

INTRODUCTION.

ON One of thofe fine Evenings that are fo rarely to be found in *England*, the Young *Chevalier D'Aumont*, related to the Duke of that Name, was taking the Air in *Somerfet-Houfe-Garden*, and enjoying the cool Breeze from the River; which after the hotteft Day that had been known that Summer, prov'd very refrefhing. He had made an Intimacy with Sir *Charles Lovemore*, a Perfon of admirable good Senfe and Knowledge, and who was now walking in the

B   Gar-

Garden with him, when *D'Aumont* leaning over the Wall, pleas'd with obferving the Rays of the Setting Sun upon the *Thames*, chang'd the Difcourfe; Dear *Lovemore*, fays the *Chevalier*, now the Ambaffador is engag'd elfewhere, what hinders me to have the entire Command of this Garden? If you think it a proper Time to perform your Promife, I will command the Door-keepers, that they fuffer none to enter here this Evening, to difturb our Converfation. Sir *Charles* having agreed to the Propofal, and Orders being accordingly given, Young *D'Aumont* re-affumed the Difcourfe: Condemn not my Curiofity, faid he, when it puts me upon enquiring after the ingenious Women of your Nation: Wit and Senfe is fo powerful a Charm, that I am not afhamed to tell you my Heart was infenfible to all the fine Ladies of the Court of *France*, and had perhaps ftill remain'd fo, if I had not been foftned by the Charms of Madam *Dacier*'s Converfation; a Woman without either Youth or Beauty, yet who makes a Thoufand Conquefts, and preferves them too. I have often admir'd her Learning, anfwer'd *Lovemore*, and to fuch a Degree, that if the War had not prevented me, I had doubtlefs gone to *France* to have feen amongft other Curiofities, a Lady who has made her felf admired

mired by all the World: But I do not imagine my Heart would have been in any Danger by that Visit, her Qualifications are of the Sort that strike the Mind, in which the Sense of Love can have but little Part: Talking to Her is conversing with an admirable Scholar, a judicious Critick, but what has That to do with the Heart? If she be as *unhandsom* as Fame reports her, and as *learned,* I should never raise my Thoughts higher than if I were discoursing with some Person of my own Sex, great and extraordinary in his Way. You are, I find, a Novice, answer'd *D'Aumont* in what relates to Women; there is no being pleas'd in their Conversation without a Mixture of the Sex which will still be mingling it self in all we say. Some other Time I will give you a Proof of this, and do my self the Honour to entertain you with certain Memoirs relating to Madam *Dacier*, of the Admiration and Applause she has gain'd, and the Conquests she has made; by which you will find, that the *Royal Academy* are not the only Persons that have done her Justice; for whereas they bestow'd but the Prize of Eloquence, others have bestow'd their Heart: I must agree with you, that her Perfections are not of the Sort that inspire immediate Delight, and warm the Blood with Pleasure, as those

4   INTRODUCTION.

do who treat well of Love: I have not known any of the Moderns in that Point come up to your famous Author of the *Atalantis*. She has carried the Passion farther than could be readily conceiv'd: Her *Germanicus on the Embroider'd Bugle Bed, naked out of the Bath :*— Her *Young and innocent Charlot,* transported with the powerful *Emotion of a just kindling Flame, sinking with Delight and Shame upon the Bosom of her Lover in the Gallery of Books :* Chevalier Tomaso *dying at the Feet of Madam* de Bedamore, *and afterwards possessing Her in that* Sylvan *Scene of Pleasure the Garden*; are such Representatives of Nature, that must warm the coldest Reader; it raises high Ideas of the Dignity of Human Kind, and informs us that we have in our Composition, wherewith to taste sublime and transporting Joys: After perusing her Inchanting Descriptions, which of us have not gone in Search of Raptures which she every where tells us, as happy Mortals, we are capable of tasting. But have we found them, *Chevalier,* answer'd his Friend? For my Part, I believe they are to be met with no where else but in her own Embraces. That is what I would experience, reply'd *D'Aumont,* if she have but half so much of the Practic, as the Theory, in the Way of Love, she must certainly be a most accomplish'd

INTRODUCTION. 5

complish'd Perfon: You have promifed to tell me what you know of her Life and Conduct; I would have her Mind, her Perfon, her Manner defcrib'd to me; I would have you paint her with as mafterly an Hand, as fhe has painted others, that I may know her perfectly before I fee her.

IS not this being a little too particular, anfwer'd Sir *Charles*, touching the Form of a Lady, who is no longer young, and was never a Beauty? Not in the leaft, briskly reply'd the Chevalier, provided her Mind and her Paffions are not in Decay. What youthful Charmer of the Sex ever pleas'd to that Height, as did Madam the Dutchefs of *Mazarin*, even to her Death; tho' I am told fhe was near twice *Rivella*'s Age? Were not all Eyes, all Hearts, devoted to her, even to the laft? One of the moft lovely Princes of the Court reduc'd himfelf almoft to Beggary, only, to fhare with others, in thofe Delights which fhe was capable of difpenfing? Laft Night I heard Mr. *C----* difcourfing of her Power; he was marry'd, as you know, to a Lady perfectly Beautiful, of the Age of Sixteen, who has fet a Thoufand Hearts on Fire; and yet he tells you, one Night with Madam *Mazarin* made him happier, than the whole Sex could do befides; which
pro-

6 INTRODUCTION.

proceeded only (as himself remarks) from her being entirely Mistress of the Art of Love; and yet she has never given the World such Testimonies of it, as has *Rivella*, by her Writings: Therefore, once more, my dearest Friend, as you have, by your own Confession, been long of her intimate Acquaintance, oblige me with as many Particulars relating to her Life and Behaviour as you can possibly recollect. By this time, the two *Cavaliers* were near one of the Benches; upon which reposing themselves, Sir *Charles Lovemore*, who perceiv'd young *D'Aumont* was prepar'd with the utmost Attention to hearken to what he should speak, began his Discourse in this manner.

THE
HISTORY
OF
RIVELLA.

THERE are so many Things Praise, and yet Blame-worthy, in *Rivella*'s Conduct, that as Her Friend, I know not well how with a good Grace, to repeat, or as yours, to conceal, because you seem to expect from me an Impartial History. Her Vertues are her own, her Vices occasion'd by her Misfortunes; and yet as I have often heard her say, *If she had been a Man, she had been without Fault:* But the Charter of that Sex being much more confin'd than ours, what is not a Crime in Men is scandalous and unpardonable in Woman, as she her
self

self has very well obferv'd in divers Places, throughout her own Writings.

HER Perfon is neither tall nor fhort; from her Youth fhe was inclin'd to Fat; whence I have often heard her Flatterers liken her to the *Grecian Venus*. It is certain, confidering that Difadvantage, fhe has the moft eafy Air that one can have; her Hair is of a pale Afh-colour, fine, and in a large Quantity. I have heard her Friends lament the Difafter of her having had the Small-pox in fuch an injurious manner, being a beautiful Child before that Diftemper; but as that Difeafe has now left her Face, fhe has fcarce any Pretence to it. Few, who have only beheld her in Publick, could be brought to like her; whereas none that became acquainted with her, could refrain from loving her. I have heard feveral Wives and Miftreffes accufe her of Fafcination: They would neither truft their Husbands, Lovers, Sons, nor Brothers with her Acquaintance upon Terms of the greateft Advantage. Speak to me of her Eyes, interrupted the *Chevalier*, you feem to have forgot that Index of the Mind; Is there to be found in them, Store of thofe animating Fires with which Her Writings are fill'd? Do Her Eyes love as well as Her Pen? You reprove me very juftly, anfwer'd the Baronet, *Rivella* would have

Of RIVELLA.

have a good deal of Reason to complain of me, if I should silently pass over the best Feature in her Face. In a Word, you have your self described them: Nothing can be more tender, ingenious and brillant with a Mixture so languishing and sweet, when Love is the Subject of the Discourse, that without being severe, we may very well conclude, the softer Passions have their Predominancy in Her Soul.

HOW are Her Teeth and Lips, spoke the *Chevalier*? Forgive me, dear *Lovemore*, for breaking in so often upon your Discourse; but Kissing being the sweetest leading Pleasure, 'tis impossible a Woman can charm without a good Mouth. Yet, answer'd *Lovemore*, I have seen very great Beauties please, as the common Witticism speaks, *in spight of their Teeth:* I do not find but Love in the general is well natur'd and civil, willing to compound for some Defects, since he knows that 'tis very difficult and rare to find true Symmetry and all Perfections in one Person: Red Hair, Out-Mouth, thin and livid Lips, black broken Teeth, course ugly Hands, long Thumbs, ill form'd dirty Nails, flat, or very large Breasts, splay Feet; which together makes a frightful Composition, yet divided amongst several, prove no Allay to the strongest Passions:

But to do *Rivella* Justice, till she grew fat, there was not I believe any Defect to be found in her Body: Her Lips admirably colour'd; Her Teeth small and even, a Breath always sweet; Her Complexion fair and fresh; yet with all this you must be us'd to her before she can be thought thoroughly agreeable. Her Hands and Arms have been publickly celebrated; it is certain, that I never saw any so well turned: Her Neck and Breasts have an establish'd Reputation for Beauty and Colour: Her Feet small and pretty. Thus I have run thro' whatever Custom suffers to be visible to us; and upon my Word, *Chevalier*, I never saw any of *Rivella*'s hidden Charms.

PARDON me this once, said *D'Aumont*, and I assure you, dear Sir *Charles*, I will not hastily interrupt you again, What Humour is she of? Is her Manner Gay or Serious? Has she Wit in her Conversation as well as Her Pen? What do you call Wit, answer'd *Lovemore*: If by that Word, you mean a Succession of such Things as can bear Repetition, even down to Posterity? How few are there of such Persons, or rather none indeed, that can be always witty? *Rivella* speaks Things pleasantly; her Company is entertaining to the last; no Woman except one's Mistress wearies one so little as her self; Her Knowledge

Of RIVELLA.

ledge is universal; she discourses well, and agreeably upon all Subjects, bating a little Affectation, which nevertheless becomes her admirably well; yet this thing is to be commended in her, that she rarely speaks of her own Writings, unless when she wou'd expresly ask the Judgment of her Friends, insomuch that I was well pleas'd at the Character a certain Person gave her (who did not mean it much to Her Advantage) that one might discourse Seven Years together with *Rivella*, and never find out from her self, that she was a *Wit*, or an *Author*.

I HAVE one Pardon more to ask you, cry'd the *Chevalier* (in a Manner that fully accus'd himself for Breach of Promise) Is she genteel? She is easy, answer'd his Friend, which is as much as can be expected from the *en bonne Point*: Her Person is always nicely clean, and Her Garb fashionable.

WHAT we say in respect of the fair Sex, I find goes for little, persu'd the *Chevalier*, I'll change my Promise of Silence with your Leave, Sir *Charles*, into Conditions of interrupting you when ever I am more than ordinarily pleas'd with what you say, and therefore do now begin with telling you, that I find my self resolved to be be in Love with *Rivella*. I eafily forgive Want of Beauty in her Face, to the Charms you tell me are in her Perfon: I hope there are no hideous Vices in her Mind, to deform the fair Idea you have given me of fine Hands and Arms, a beautiful Neck and Breaft, pretty Feet, and, I take it for granted, Limbs that make up the Symmetry of the whole.

RIVELLA is certainly much indebted, continu'd *Lovemore*, to a Liberal Education, and thofe early Precepts of Vertue taught her and practifed in her Father's Houfe. There was then fuch a Foundation laid, that tho' Youth, Misfortunes, and Love, for feveral Years have interrupted fo fair a Building, yet fome Time fince, fhe is returned with the greateft Application to repair that Lofs and Defect; if not with relation to this World (where Women have found it impoffible to be reinftated) yet of the next, which has mercifully told us, *Mankind can commit no Crimes but what upon Converfion may be forgiven.*

RIVELLA's natural Temper is haughty, impatient of Contradiction: She is nicely tenacious of the Privilege of Her own Sex, in Point of what Refpect ought to be paid by ours to the Ladies; and as fhe underftands good Breeding to a Punctuali-

ty,

ty, tho' the Freedom of her Humour often dispenses with *Forms*, she will not easily forgive what Person soever shall be wanting in that which Custom has made her Due: Her Soul is soft and tender to the Afflicted, her Tears wait upon their Misfortunes, and there is nothing she does not do to asswage them. You need but tell her a Person is in Misery to engage her Concern, her Purse, and her Interest in their Behalf: I have often heard her say, that she *was an utter Stranger to what is meant by Hatred and Revenge*; nor was she ever known to persue hers upon any Person, tho' often injured, excepting Mr. *S——le*, whose notorious Ingratitude and Breach of Friendship affected her too far, and made her think it the highest Piece of Justice to expose him.

NOW I have done with her Person, I fear you will think me too particular in my Description of her Mind: But *Chevalier* there lies the intrinsick Value; 'tis that which either accomplishes or deforms a Person. I will in few Words conclude her Character; she has lov'd Expence, even to being extravagant, which in a Woman of Fortune might more justly have been term'd Generosity: She is Grateful, unalterable in those Principles of Loyalty, derived from her Family: A little too vainglorious

glorious of those Perfections which have been ascribed to her; she does not however boast of what Praise, or Favours, Persons of Rank may have conferr'd upon her: She loves *Truth*, and has too often given her self the Liberty to *speak*, as well as *write* it.

SHE was born in *Hampshire*, in one of those Islands, which formerly belong'd to *France*, where her Father was Governour; afterwards he enjoy'd the same Post in other Places in *England*. He was the Second Son of an Ancient Family; the better Part of the Estate was ruin'd in the Civil War by adhering to the *Royal Family*, without ever being repair'd, or scarce taken Notice of, at the Restoration: The Governour was Brave, full of Honour, and a very fine Gentleman: He became a Scholar in the Midst of a Camp, having left the University at Sixteen Years of Age, to follow the Fortunes of K. *Charles* the First. His Temper had too much of the Stoick in it for the Good of his Family. After a Life the best Part spent in Civil and foreign War, he began to love Ease and Retirement, devoting himself to his Study, and the Charge of his little Post, without ever following the Court: His great Vertue and Modesty render'd him unfit for folliciting such Persons, by whom Preferment was there to be gain'd; so that his
De-

Deserts seem'd bury'd and forgotten. In his Solitude he wrote several Tracts for his own Amusement; his *Latin Commentaries* of the *Civil Wars of England*, having pass'd through *Europe*, may perhaps have reach'd your Notice, which is all that I shall mention to you of his Writings, because you are unacquainted with our *English* State of Learning; and yet upon recollection, since the *Turkish-Spy* has been translated into other Languages, I must likewise tell you that our Governour was the Genuine Author of the first Volume of that admir'd and successful Work. An Ingenious *Physician*, related to the Family by Marriage, had the Charge of looking over his Papers amongst which he found that Manuscript, which he easily reserved to his proper Use; and both by his own Pen, and the assistance of some others, continu'd the Work until the Eighth Volume, without ever having the Justice to Name the Author of the First.

BUT this is little relating to the Adventures of *Rivella*, who had the Misfortune to be Born with an indifferent Beauty, between two Sisters perfectly Handsom; and yet, as I have often thought my self, and as I have heard others say, they had less Power over Mankind than had *Rivella*. *Maria* the eldest, was unhappily bestow'd bestow'd in Marriage, (at her own Request, by her Father's fondness and assent to his Daughter's Choice) on a Wretch every way unworthy of Her, of her Fortune, her Birth, her Charms or Tenderness.

MY Father's Estate lay very near *Rivella*'s Father's Government. I was then a Youth, who took a great deal of Delight in going to the Castle, where Three such fair Persons were inclosed.

THE eldest was now upon her Marriage. *Cordelia* the youngest scarce yet thought of. *Rivella* had just reach'd the Age of Twelve, when I beheld the wonderful Effects of Love upon the Heart of young and innocent Persons. I had used to please my self in talking Romantick Stories to her, and with furnishing her with Books of that Strain. The Fair *Maria* was six Years elder, and above my Hopes; I was a meer Lad, as yet unfashion'd; I beheld her with Admiration, as we do a glorious Sky; it is not yet our Hemisphere, nor do we think of shining there. *Rivella* was nearer to my Age and Understanding, and tho' four Years younger than my self, was the Wittiest Girl in the World: I would have kiss'd her, and embrac'd her a thousand Times over,

Of RIVELLA.

over, but had no Opportunity. Never any young Ladies had so severe an Education: They had lost their Mother when very young, and their Father, who had past many Years abroad, during the Exile of the *Royal Family* had brought into *England* with him all the Jealousy and Distrust of the *Spaniard* and *Italian*. I have often heard *Rivella* regret her having never gone to School, as losing the innocent Play and Diversions of those of her own Age. A severe *Governante*, worse than any *Duenna*, forbid all Approaches to the Appartment of the Fair; as young as I was, I could only be admitted at Dinner or Supper, when our Family visited; but never alone: She was fond of Scribling: Tho' in so tender an Age, she wrote Verses, which considering her Youth were pardonable, since they might very well be read without Disgust; but there was something surprizing in her Letters; so natural, so spirituous, so sprightly, so well turned, that from the first to the last I must and ever will maintain, that all her other Productions however successful they have been, come short of her Talent in writing Letters: I have had Numbers of them; my Servant us'd to wait on her as if to bring her Books to read, in the Cove of which I had contrived always to send her a Note, which she return'd turn'd in the same Manner. But this was perfect Fooling; I lov'd her, but she did not return my Passion, yet without any affected Coyness, or personating a Heroine of the many Romances she daily read. *Rivella* would let me know in the very best Language, with a bewitching Air of Sincerity and Manners, that she was not really cruel, but insensible; that I had hitherto fail'd of inspiring her with new Thoughts: Since her young Heart was not conscious of any Alteration in my Favour; but in return to that generous Concern I express'd for her, she would instruct it as much as possible to be gratefull; 'till when my Letters, and the Pleasure of writing to me again, was a Diversion more to her Taste than any she met with besides; and therefore would not deny her self the Satisfaction of hearing from, or of answering me, as often as she had an Opportunity.

BUT all my Hopes of touching her Heart were suddenly blasted. To bring my self back to what I was just now telling you of the strange Effects of Love in youthful Hearts, I must acquaint you that upon the Report of an Invasion from *Holland*, a Supply of Forces was sent to the Garrison, amongst which was a *Subaltern* Officer, the most beautiful Youth I remember

ber to have ever seen, till I beheld the Chevalier *D'Aumont*; Monsieur *D' Aumont* told Sir *Charles*, with a Smile, his Compliment should not procure him a Pause in his relation, and therefore conjur'd him to proceed.

THIS Young Fellow, pursu'd *Lovemore*, had no other Pretences but those of his Person, to qualify him for being my Rival; neither of himself did he dream of becoming such; he durst not presume to lift up his Eyes to the Favourite Daughter of the *Governour*; but alas! hers descended to fix themselves on him: I have heard her declare since, that tho' she had read so much of Love, and that I had often spoke to her of it in my Letters, yet she was utterly ignorant of what it was, till she felt his fatal Power; nay after she had felt it, she scarce guess'd at her Disease, till she found her Cure: Young *Lysander*, for so was my Rival call'd, knew not how to receive a good Fortune, which was become so obvious, that even her Father and all the Company perceiv'd her Distemper better than her self: Her Eyes were continually fix'd upon this young Warrior, she could neither eat nor sleep; she became Hectick, and had all the Symptoms of a dangerous Indisposition. They caus'd her to be let Blood, which joyn'd to her Abstinence from Food, made her but the weaker, whilst her Distemper grew more strong. The Gentleman who had newly married her Sister, was of Counsel with the Family how to suppress this growing Misfortune; he spoke roundly to the *Youth*, who had no Thoughts of improving the Opportunity, and charg'd him not to give in to the Follies of the young Girl; he told him he would shoot him thro' the Head if he attempted any thing towards soothing *Rivella's* Prepossession, or rather Madness. *Lysander* who was passionately in Love elsewhere, easily assured them he had no Designs upon that very young Lady, and would decline all Opportunities of entertaining her; but as the *Governour*'s hospitable Table made most Persons welcom, he forbore not to pursue his first Invitation, and came often to Dinner where the dear little Creature saw him constantly, and never removed her Eyes from his Face: His Voice was very good; the Songs then in Vogue amorous, and such as suited her Temper of Mind; she drank the Poyson both at her Ears and Eyes, and never took Care to manage, or conceal her Passion; possibly what she has since told me in that Point was true, That *She knew not what she did, as not having Freewill, or the Benefit of Reflection; nor could she consider any Thing but* Lysander, *tho' amidst a Croud.*

THE *Governour* was a wife Man, and forbore saying any Thing to the Girl which might acquaint her with her own Distemper, much less cause her to suspect that himself and others were acquainted with it: He caress'd her more than usual, sooth'd and lamented her Indisposition, proposed Change of Air to her; she fell a weeping, and begg'd she might not go to be sick from under his Care, for that would certainly break her Heart: He thought gentle Methods were the best, and therefore order'd her Sisters, and their Governess, to do all they could to divert, but never to leave her alone with young *Lysander*.

IN the mean Time, by the Interest the *Governour* made at Court, he procured that Battalion to be recall'd, and another to be deputed in Place of what had given him so much Uneasiness. The Day before their Marching Orders came; he proposed playing after Dinner for an Hour or Two at *Hazard*; most of the Gentlemen present were willing to entertain the *Governour*. *Lysander* excused himself, as having lost the last Night, all his small Stock at *Back-Gammon*; his little Mistress heard this with a vast Concern; and as she afterwards told me, could have readily bestow'd upon

upon him all she had of value in the World. Her Father, who beheld her in a deep *Resvery*, with her Eyes fix'd intently upon *Lysander*, call'd her to him, and giving her a Key where his Money was kept, order'd her to fetch him a certain Sum to Play with; she obey'd, but no sooner beheld the glittering Store, (without reflecting on what might be the Consequence, or indeed any Thing else but that her Dear *Lysander* wanted Money) than she dipt her little Hand into an Hundred Pound Bag full of Guineas, and drew thence as much as it would hold: Upon her return she met him in the Gallery; (seeing the Company ingag'd in Play he was stolen off, possibly with an intent to follow *Rivella*, and have a Moment to speak to her in without Witnesses; for the Regards he gave her from his Eyes, when he durst encounter Hers, spoke him wiling to be Grateful) She bid him hold out his Hat and say nothing, then throwing in the Spoil, she briskly pass'd on to the Company, brought her Father the Money he wanted; return'd him the Key, and set her self down to overlook the Gamesters.

THIS Story I have had from her self, by which Action she was since convinc'd of the Greatness of her Prepossession, being perfectly Just by Nature, Principle, and
Edu-

Education, nothing but Love, and that in a high degree could have made her otherwise. The Awe she was in of her Father was so great, that upon the highest Emergency she would not, durst not have wrong'd him of a single Shilling. Whether the *Governour* never miss'd those Guineas, as having always a great deal of Money by him for the Garrison's Subsistence; or that he was too wise to speak of a Thing that would have reflected upon his Daughter's Credit; *Rivella* was so Happy as to hear no more of it?

MEAN time my Affair went on but Ill; She answer'd none of my Letters, nay forgot to read them; when I came to visit her, she shew'd me a Pocket full which she had never open'd; this vex'd me excessively, and the more, when she suffer'd me with extream Indifference to take them again: I would have known the Reason of this Alteration; she cou'd not account for it, so that I left her with outward Rage, but inwardly my Heart was more her Slave than before: Whether it be the vile and sordid Nature of the God of Love to make us mostly doat upon ungenerous Usage, and at other Times to cause us to return with equal Ingratitude the Kindness we meet from others.

THE

The HISTORY

THE next Day I ingag'd my Sister to make a Visit to the Castle; we took the Cool of the Morning, she was intimate with *Maria* before her Marriage, and suffer'd her self to be persuaded to let me wait on her; we were drinking Chocolate at the *Governour*'s Toilet, where *Rivella* and her Sisters attended; when the Drums beat a loud Alarm, we were presently told we should see a very fine Sight, the New Forces march in, and the Old ones out, if they can properly be call'd so, that had not been there above Eighteen Days; at the News my Mistress, who had heard nothing of it before, began to turn pale as Death; she ran to her *Papa*, and falling upon his Bosom, wept and sob'd with such Vehemence, that he apprehended she was falling into Hysterick Fits. Her Father sent for their Governess to carry her to her Bed-Chamber, but she hung upon him in such a Manner, that without doing her a great deal of Violence, they could not remove her thence. I ran to her Assistance with a Wonder great as my Concern, but she more particularly rejected my Touches, and all that I could say for her Consolation.

MEAN time the Commander in chief, followed by most of his Officers (amongst which

Of RIVELLA. 25

which the lovely *Lysander* appeared with a languishing Air full of Disappointment, which yet added to his Beauty) came up to the *Governour*, and told him his Men were all under Arms and ready to march forth, whenever he pleas'd to give the Word of Command. At the same Time entred another Gentleman equally attended, whom the *Governour* stept forth to welcome: He assured him the Forces that obey'd him were all drawn up upon the *Counterscarp*, and thought themselves happy, more particularly himself, to have the good Fortune of being quarter'd where a Person of such Honour and Humanity was *Governour*.

TO conclude, poor *Rivella* fell from one Fainting into another without the least immodest Expression, Glance or Discovery of what had occasion'd her Fright: She was remov'd, and we had the Satisfaction of seeing the military Change of Forces, and poor *Lysander* depart without ever beholding his Mistress more.

METHINKS, Monsieur *le Chevalier*, continu'd *Lovemore*, I am too fond of such Particularities as made up the first Scene of my Unhappiness: I call it so, when I remember how dangerously ill that poor Girl grew, and how my Soul sickned at her Danger. What avails it to renew past Pains or Pleasures? *Rivella* recover'd, and begg'd she might be remov'd for some Time to any other Place, which would perhaps better agree with her than the Air wherein I breath'd. In a Word, without ever having been belov'd, my Importunities now caused me to be for some Time even hated by Her.

THE Lady had a younger Brother who was pension'd at a *Hugenot* Minister's House on the other Side of the Sea and Country, about eighteen Miles farther from *London*, a Solitude rude and barbarous: *Rivella* begg'd to be sent thither, that she might improve Time, and learn *French:* She would not have any Servant with her for fear of talking *English*; nor would she ever speak to her Brother in that Language: What shall I say, so incredible was her Application, tho' she had a Relapse of her former Distemper, that in three Months Time she was instructed so far as to read, speak and write *French* with a Perfection truly wonderful; insomuch that when her Father came to take her home, finding the Air had very much impair'd her Health, the good *Minister*, her Master, who was a learned and modest Person, begg'd the *Governour* to leave *Mademoiselle* with him, and he would engage in twelve Months, counting from the Time she first came, to make her Mistress

of

of those Four Languages of which he was Master, *viz. Latin, French, Spanish* and *Italian*.

THE next Day after her Return, I came to pay my Duty to her, and welcome her back; she was less averse, but not more tender: The Respect I had for her, made me forbear to reproach her with the Passion she had shewn for *Lysander*; my Sisters tattling with her Sisters, had gain'd the Secret, and very little to my Ease imparted the Confidence to me: We began an Habit of Friendship on her Side, tho' on mine it never ceased to be Love: And I may very truly tell you, *Chevalier*, that such was the Effect of that early Disappointment, as has for ever hinder'd me from knowing the true Pleasures of Passion, because I have never felt a Concern for any other Woman, comparable to what I felt for *Rivella*.

AFTER this short Absence, I found my self condemn'd to a more lasting one: My Father design'd to send me abroad with an Intent that I might spend some Years in my Travel. At the same Time *Rivella* had the Promise of the next Vacancy for Maid of Honour to the Queen: I congratulated her good Fortune, acquainting her with my ill Fortune in being condemn'd to separate my self from her.

Tho' I was never happy in her Love, yet I was jealous of losing her Friendship, amidst the Diversions of a Court, and the Dangers of Absence: Who does not know the Fervency of our early Passions? I begg'd to secure her to me, by a Marriage unknown to our Parents, but I could not prevail with her; she fear'd to displease her Father, and I durst not ask the Consent of mine: I had flatter'd my self that it was much easier to gain their Pardon than procure their Approbation, because we were both so young: But *Rivella* was immoveable, notwithstanding all I could say to her. How often for her Sake, have I lamented her Disdain, and little Foresight, for refusing to marry me, which had she agreed to, all those Misfortunes that have since attended her, in Point of Honour and the World's Opinion, had probably been prevented, which shews there is something in what the vulgar conceive, of *its being once in our Lives in our own Power to make or assist our Fortune.*

I departed for *Italy*; the *Abdication* immediately came on, the Queen was gone to *France*, and *Rivella* thereby disappointed of going to Court. Her Father was what he term'd himself, truly loyal; he laid down his Command and retired with his Family, to a private Life, and a small
Country-

Of RIVELLA.

Country-House, where the Misfortunes of his Royal Master sunk so deep into his Thoughts, that he dy'd soon after, in mortal Apprehension of what would befall his unhappy Country.

HERE begins *Rivella*'s real Misfortunes; it would be well for her, that I could say here she dy'd with Honour, as did her Father: I must refer you to her own Story, under the Name of *Delia*, in the *Atalantis*, for the next Four miserable Years of her Life: My self did not return from Travel in three Years: My Father was also dead, and left me a fair Estate without any Incumbrance; my Sister having been married some time before. I heard this News when I was upon my return, resolving to offer *Rivella* my whole Fortune, as she was already possessed of my Heart: Absence, nor the Conversation of other Women had not supplanted her in my Esteem. When I thought of her Genius and sprightly Wit, Comparison indear'd her to me the more; but I was extreamly griev'd and disappointed, when I learn'd her ruin. I will not tell you how much I was touch'd with it. I sought her out with Obstinacy; but could not tell where to meet her: I was almost a Year in the Search, and then gave it over; till one Night I happen'd to call in at Madam *Mazarin*'s, where I saw *Rivella* introduc'd by by *Hilaria,* a Royal Miſtreſs of one of our preceding Kings. I ſhook my Head in beholding her in ſuch Company. I was ſo much improv'd by Travelling, that, as ſhe told me afterwards, She did not know me 'till I had ſpoken to her: I could not ſay the ſame thing of her. She was much impair'd; her ſprightly Air, in which lay her greateſt Charm, was turn'd into a languiſhing Melancholy; the white of her Skin, degenerated into a yellowiſh Hue, occaſion'd by her Misfortunes, and three Years Solitude; tho' quickly after ſhe recover'd both her Air and her Complexion.

HOW confus'd and abaſh'd ſhe was at my addreſſing to her! The Freedom of the Place gave me Opportunity to ſay what I pleas'd to her: She was not one of the Gameſters, but begg'd me I would be pleas'd to retire, and ſpare her the Shame of an *Eclairciſment* in a Place no way proper for ſuch an Affair. I obey'd, and accepted the Offer ſhe made me of ſupping with her at *Hilaria*'s Houſe, where at preſent ſhe was lodg'd; that Lady having ſeldom the Power of returning home from Play before Morning, unleſs upon a very ill Run, when ſhe chanced to loſe her Money ſooner than ordinary.

NEVER was there a more desolate Meeting than between my self and *Rivella*: She told me all her Misfortunes with an Air so perfectly ingenuous, that, if some Part of the World who were not acquainted with her Vertue, ridicul'd her Marriage, and the Villany of her Kinsman; I, who knew her Sincerity, could not help believing all she said. My Tears were Witnesses of my Grief; it was not in my Power to say any thing to lessen her's: I therefore left her abruptly, without being able to eat or drink any thing with her for that Night.

TIME, which allays all our Passions, lessen'd the Sorrow I felt for *Rivella*'s Ruin, and even made me an Advocate to asswage hers: The Diversions of the House she was in were dangerous Restoratives: Her Wit, and Gaity of Temper return'd, but not her Innocence.

HILARIA had met with *Rivella* in her solitary Mansion, visiting a Lady who liv'd next Door to the poor Recluse. She was the only Person that in three Years *Rivella* had convers'd with, and that but since her Husband was gone into the Country: Her Story was quickly known. *Hilaria*, passionately fond of new Faces, of which Sex soever, us'd a thousand Arguments

ments to dissuade her from wearing away her Bloom in Grief and Solitude. She read her a learned Lecture upon the Ill-nature of the World, that wou'd never restore a Woman's Reputation, how innocent soever she really were, if Appearances prov'd to be against her; therefore she gave her Advice, which she did not disdain to Practise; the *English* of which was, *To make her self as happy as she could without valuing or regretting those, by whom it was impossible to be valu'd.*

THE Lady, at whose House *Rivella* first became acquainted with *Hilaria*, perceiv'd her Indiscretion in bringing them together. The Love of Novelty, as usual, so far prevail'd, that herself was immediately discarded, and *Rivella* perswaded to take up her Residence near *Hilaria*'s; which made her so inveterate an Enemy to *Rivella*, that the first great Blow struck against her Reputation, proceeded from that Woman's malicious Tongue: She was not contented to tell all Persons, who began to know and esteem *Rivella*, that her Marriage was a Cheat, but even sent Letters by the Penny-Post to make *Hilaria* jealous of *Rivella's* Youth, in respect of him who at that time happen'd to be her Favourite.

Of RIVELLA.

RIVELLA has often told me, That from *Hilaria* she receiv'd the first ill Impressions of Count *Fortunatus*, touching his Ingratitude, Immorality, and Avarice; being her self an Eye-Witness when he deny'd *Hilaria* (who had given him Thousands) the common Civility of lending her Twenty Guineas at *Basset*; which, together with betraying his Master, and raising himself by his Sister's Dishonour, she had always esteem'd a just and flaming Subject for Satire.

RIVELLA had now reign'd six Months in *Hilaria*'s Favour, an Age to one of her inconstant Temper; when that Lady found out a new Face to whom the old must give Place, and such a one, of whom she could not justly have any Jealousie in point of Youth or Agreeableness; the Person I speak of, was a Kitchin-maid married to her Master, who had been refug'd with King *James* in *France*. He dy'd, and left her what he had, which was quickly squander'd at Play; but she gain'd Experience enough by it to make Gaming her Livelihood, and return'd into *England* with the monstrous Affectation of calling her self a *French-woman*; her Dialect being thence-forward nothing but a sort of broken *English*: This passed upon the Town, because her Original was so obscure, that they were unacquainted with it. She generally ply'd at Madam *Mazarin*'s *Basset-*Table, and was also of use to her in Affairs of Pleasure; but whether that Lady grew weary of her Impertinence, and strange ridiculous Airs, or that she thought *Hilaria* might prove a better Bubble; she profited of the Advances that were made her, and accepted of an Invitation to come and take up her Lodging at *Hilaria*'s House, where in a few Months she repay'd the Civility that had been shewn her, by clapping up a clandestine Match between her Patroness's eldest Son, a Person tho' of weak Intellects, yet of great Consideration, and a young Lady of little or no Fortune.

BUT to return to *Rivella*. *Hilaria* was tir'd, and resolv'd to take the first Opportunity to be rude to her: She knew her Spirit would not easily forgive any Point of Incivility or Disrespect.

HILARIA was *Querilous, Fierce, Loquacious*, excessively fond, or infamously rude: When she was disgusted with any Person, she never fail'd to reproach them with all the Bitterness and Wit she was Mistress of, with such Malice and Ill-nature, that she was hated not only by all the World, but by her own Children and Fa-

Of *RIVELLA*.

Family; not one of her Servants, but what would have laugh'd to see her lie dead amongst them, how affecting soever such Objects are in any other Case. The Extreams of *Prodigality*, and *Covetousness*; of *Love* and *Hatred*; of *Dotage* and *Aversion*, were joyn'd together in *Hilaria*'s Soul.

RIVELLA may well call it her second great Misfortune to have been acquainted with that Lady, who, to excuse her own Inconstancy, always blasted the Character of those whom she was grown weary of, as if by *Slander* and *Scandal*, she could take the Odium from her self, and fix it upon others.

SOME few Days before *Hilaria* was resolved to part with *Rivella*, to make Room for the Person who was to succeed her; she pretended a more than ordinary Passion, caused her to quit her Lodgings to come and take part of her own Bed. *Rivella* attributed this *Feint* of Kindness to the Lady's Fears, lest she should see the Man *Hilaria* was in Love with, at more Ease in her own House than when she was in hers; tho' that beloved Person had always a Hatred and Distrust of *Rivella*. He kept a Mistress in the next Street, in as much Grandeur as his Lady: He fear'd she

she would come to the Knowledge of it by this new and young Favourite, whose Birth and Temper put her above the Hopes of bringing her into his Interest, as he took care all others should be that approached *Hilaria*. He resolved, how dishonourable soever the Procedure were, to ruin *Rivella*, for fear she should ruin him; and therefore told his Lady she had made Advances to him, which for her Ladyship's sake he had rejected; this agreed with the unknown Intelligence that had been sent by the Penny-Post; but because she was not yet provided with any Lady that would be her Favourite in *Rivella*'s Place; she took no notice of her Fears, but politickly chose to give her a great and lovely Amusement; it was with one of her own Sons, whom she caress'd more than usual to draw him oftner to her House, leaving them alone together upon such plausible Pretences, as seem'd the Effect of Accident not Design: What might have proceeded from so dangerous a Temptation, I dare not presume to determine, because *Hilaria* and *Rivella*'s Friendship immediately broke off upon the Assurance the former had receiv'd from the broken *French-woman*, that she would come and supply her Place.

THE last Day she was at *Hilaria*'s House, just as they sat down to Dinner, Ri-

Of RIVELLA

Rivella was told that her Sister *Maria*'s Husband was fallen into great Distress, which so sensibly affected her, that she could eat nothing; she sent Word to a Friend, who could give her an Account of the whole Matter, that she would wait upon her at Six a Clock at Night, resolving not to lose that Post, if it were true that her Sister was in Misfortune, without sending her some Relief. After Dinner several Ladies came in to Cards; *Hilaria* ask'd *Rivella* to play; she begg'd Her Ladyship's Excuse, because she had Business at Six a Clock; they persuaded her to play for Two Hours, which accordingly she did, and then had a Coach sent for and return'd not till Eight: She had been inform'd abroad that Matters were very well compos'd touching her Sister's Affairs, which extreamly lightned her Heart; she came back in a very good Humour, and very hungry, which she told *Hilaria*, who, with Leave of the first Dutchess in *England* that was then at Play, order'd Supper to be immediately got ready, for that her dear *Rivella* had eat nothing all Day: As soon as they were set to Table, *Rivella* repeated those Words again, that she was very hungry; *Hilaria* told her, she was glad of it, *There were some Things which got one a good Stomach*: *Rivella* ask'd her Ladyship what those things were?
Hilaria

Hilaria anfwer'd, 'Don't you know what?
' That which you have been doing with
' my ——— [and named her own Son,]
' Nay, don't blufh *Rivella*; 'twas doubt-
' lefs an Appointment, I faw him to Day
' kifs you as he lead you thro' the dark
' Drawing-Room down to Dinner. Your
' Ladyfhip may have feen him attempt it,
' anfwer'd *Rivella*, [perfectly frighted
with her Words,] ' and feen me refufe the
' Honour: But why [reply'd *Hilaria*] did
' you go out in a Hackney-Coach, with-
' out a Servant? Becaufe [fays *Rivella*]
' my Vifit lay a great Way off, too far
' for your Ladyfhip's Chairmen to go: It
' rain'd, and does ftill rain extreamly; I
' was tender of your Ladyfhip's Horfes
' this cold wet Night; both the Footmen
' were gone on Errands; I ask'd below
' for one of them, I was too well Man-
' ner'd to take the *Black*, and leave none
' to attend your Ladyfhip; efpecially when
' my Lady Dutchefs was here: Befides,
' your own Porter paid the Coachman,
' which was the fame I carried out with
' me;. he was forc'd to wait fome Time at
' the Gate, till a Guinea could be chang'd,
' becaufe I had no Silver; I beg all this
' good Company to judge, whether any
' Woman would be fo indifcreet, knowing
' very well, as I do, that I have one Friend
' in this Houfe, that would not fail ex-
' amining

' amining the Coachman where he had
' carried me, if it were but in hopes of
' doing me a Prejudice with the World
' and your Ladyship.'

THE Truth is, *Hilaria* was always superstitious at Play; she won whilst *Rivella* was there, and would not have her remov'd from the Place she was in, thinking she brought her good Luck: After she was gone, her Luck turn'd; so that before *Rivella* came back, *Hilaria* had lost above two hundred Guineas, which put her into a Humour to expose *Rivella* in the Manner you have heard; who briskly rose up from Table without eating any Thing, begging her Ladyship's Leave to retire, whom she knew to be so great a Mistress of Sense, as well as of good Manners, that she would never have affronted any Person at her own Table, but one whom she held unworthy of the Honour of sitting there.

NEXT Morning she wrote a Note to *Hilaria*'s Son, to desire the Favour of seeing him; he accordingly obey'd: *Rivella* desir'd him to acquaint my Lady where he was last Night, from Six till Eight; he told her at the Play in the side Box with the Duke of---- whom he would bring to justify what he said: I chanc'd chanc'd to come in to drink Tea with the Ladies; *Rivella* told me her Diſtreſs; I was mov'd at it, and the more, becauſe I had been my ſelf at the Play, and ſaw the Perſon for whom ſhe was accus'd, ſet the Play out: In a Word *Rivella* waited till *Hilaria* was viſible, and then went to take her Leave of her with ſuch an Air of Reſentment, Innocence, yet good Manners, as quite confounded the haughty *Hilaria*.

FROM that Day forwards ſhe never ſaw her more; too happy indeed if ſhe had never ſeen her: All the World was fond of *Rivella*, and enquiring for her of *Hilaria* ſhe could make no other Excuſe for her own abominable Temper, and deteſtable Inconſtancy, but that ſhe was run away with —— her Son, and probably would not have the Aſſurance ever to appear at her Houſe again.

BUT I who knew *Rivella*'s Innocency, beg'd ſhe wou'd retire to my Seat in the Country, where ſhe might be ſure to command with the ſame Power as if it were her own, as in effect it muſt be, ſince my ſelf was ſo devoted to her Service: I made her this Offer becauſe it could no longer do her an Injury in the Opinion of the World which was ſufficiently prejudic'd againſt her already; ſhe excus'd her ſelf,

self, upon telling me she must first be in Love with a Man before she thought fit to reside with him; which was not my Case, tho' she had never fail'd in Respect, Esteem and Friendship for me. She told me her Love of Solitude was improved by her Disgust of the World; and since it was impossible for her to be publick with Reputation, she was resolv'd to remain in it conceal'd: She was sorry that the War hinder'd her to go to *France*, where she had a very great Inclination to pass her Days; but since that could not be help'd, she said her Design was to waste most of her Time in *England* in Places where she was unknown. To be short, she spent Two Years in this Amusement; in all that Time never making her self acquainted at any Place where she liv'd. 'Twas in this Solitude, that she compos'd her first Tragedy, which was much more famous for the Language, Fire and Tenderness than the Conduct. Mrs. *Barry* distinguish'd her self as much as in any Part that ever she play'd. I have since often heard *Rivella* laugh and wonder that a Man of Mr. *Betterton*'s grave Sense and Judgment should think well enough of the Productions of a Woman of Eighteen, to bring it upon the Stage in so handsom a Manner as he did, when her self could hardly now bear the reading of it.

BEHOLD another wrong Step towards ruining *Rivella*'s Character with the World; the Incenſe that was daily offer'd her upon this Occaſion from the Men of Vogue and Wit: Her Appartment was daily crouded with them. There is a Copy of Verſes printed before her *Play*, ſaid to be writ by a great Hand, which they agreed to make their common Topick when they would addreſs to her. have heard them ſo often recited, that I ſtill remember them, which are thus in *Engliſh*. If you don't thorougly underſtand it, I'll give you the Words in *French*.

What! all our Sex in one ſad Hour un-
(done?
Loſt are our Arts, our Learning, our Renown,
Since Nature's Tide of Wit came roulling
(down:

Keen were your Eyes we knew, and ſure
(their Darts;
Fire to our Soul they ſend, and Paſſion to
(our Hearts!

Needleſs was an Addition to ſuch Arms,

When all Mankind were Vaſſals to your
(Charms:

That

Of RIVELLA. 43

That Hand but seen, gives Wonder and De-
(sire,

Snow to the Sight, but with its Touches
(Fire!

Who sees thy Yielding Queen, *and would*
(not be

On any Terms the blest, the happy He;

Entranc'd we fancy all his Extasie.

Quote Ovid *now no more ye amorous*
(Swains,

Delia *than* Ovid *has more moving Strains.*

Nature in Her alone exceeds all Art;

And Nature sure does nearest touch the
(Heart.

Oh! might I call the bright Discoverer mine,

The whole fair Sex unenvy'd I'd resign;

Give all my happy Hours to Delia's
(Charms,

She who by writing thus our Wishes warms,

What Worlds of Love must circle in her
(Arms?

I had still so much Concern for *Rivella*, that I pitied her Conduct, which I saw must

must infallibly center in her Ruin: There was no Language approached her Ear but Flattery and Perfuasion to Delight and Love. The Cafuifts told her a Woman of her Wit had the Privilege of the other Sex, fince all Things were pardonable to a Lady *who could fo well give Laws to others, yet was not obliged to keep them her felf.* Her Vanity was now at the Height, fo was her Gaiety and good Humour, efpecially at Meat, fhe underftood good Living, and indulged her felf in it: *Rivella* never drank but at Meals, but then it was no way loft upon her, for her Wit was never fo fparkling as when fhe was pleas'd with her Wine. I could not keep away from her Houfe, yet was ftark mad to fee her delighted with every Fop, who flatter'd her Vanity: I us'd to take the Privilege of long Acquaintance and Efteem to correct her ill Taft, and the wrong Turn fhe gave her Judgment in admitting Adulation from fuch Wretches as many of them were; tho' indeed feveral Perfons of very good Senfe allow'd *Rivella*'s Merit, and afforded her the Honour of their Converfation and Efteem: She look'd upon all I faid with an evil Eye; believing there was ftill Jealoufy at the Bottom. She did not think fit to correct a Conduct which fhe call'd very innocent, for me whofe Paffion fhe had never valu'd: I ftill preach'd,

and

and she still went on in her own Way, without any Regard to my Doctrine, till Experience gave her enough of her Indiscretion.

A certain Gentleman, who was a very great Scholar and Master of abundance of Sense and Judgment, at her own Request, brought to her Acquaintance one Sir *Peter Vainlove*, intending to do her Service as to her Design of writing for the Theater, that Person having then Interest enough to introduce upon one Stage whatever Pieces he pleas'd: This Knight had a very good Face, but his Body was grown fat: He was naturally short, and his Legs being what they call somewhat bandy, he was advis'd to wear his Cloaths very long, to help conceal that Defect; insomuch that his Dress made him look shorter than he was: He was following a handsom Lady in the *Mall*, after a World of Courtship, and begging her in vain to let him know where she liv'd; seeing she was prepared to leave the *Park* he renew'd his Efforts, offering to go down upon his Knees to her, to have her grant his Request; the Lady turn'd gravely upon him, and told him she thought, *he had been upon his Knees all this Time:* The Knight conscious of his duck Legs and long Coat, retired in the greatest Confusion, notwithstanding his natural and acquired Assurance.

rance. Sir *Peter* was supposed to be towards Fifty when he became acquainted with *Rivella*, and his Constitution broken by those Excesses, of which in his Youth he had been guilty: He was Married young to a Lady of Worth and Honour, who brought him a very large Joynture; never any Woman better deserved the Character of a good Wife, being universally obliging to all her Husband's Humours; the great Love she had for him, together with her own Sweetness of Temper, made him infinitely easy at Home; but he was detestably vain, and lov'd to be thought in the Favour of the Fair, which was indeed his only Fault, for he had a great deal of Wit and good Nature; but sure no Youth of Twenty had so vast a *Foible* for being admired. He wrote very pretty well-turned *Billet-deuxs*; he was not at all sparing of his Letters when he met a Woman that had any Knack that Way: *Rivella* was much to his Taste, so that presently there grew the greatest Intimacy in the World between them; but because he found she was a Woman of Fire, more than perhaps he could answer, he was resolved to destroy any Hopes she might have of a nearer Correspondence than would conveniently suit with his present Circumstances, by telling her his Heart was

was already prepossess'd. This served him to a double Purpose, *First*, To let her know that he was reciprocally admired: And *Secondly*, That no great things were to be expected from a Person who was engaged, or rather devoted to another. He made *Rivella* an entire Confident of his Amour, naming fine Mrs. *Settee*, then of the City, at the Head of her Six tall Daughters, not half so beautiful as their Mother: This Affair had subsisted Ten Years, according to the Knight's own Account. The Lady had begun it her self (falling in Love with him at the *Temple-Revels*) by Letters of Admiration to him; after some Time, corresponding by amorous high-flown *Billets*, she granted a Meeting, but was three Years before she would let him know who she was, tho' there were most Liberties but that of the Face allow'd. Afterwards they met without any of that Reserve: It cost the Knight according to his own Report three Hundred Pounds a Year (besides two Thousand Pounds worth of Jewels presented at Times) to see her but once a Week, and give her a Supper: He managed this Matter so much to his own vain false Reputation, that it was become a Proverb amongst his Friends, *Oh 'tis Friday Night, you must not expect to see Sir Peter!* He put a Relation of his own into a House, and maintain'd her there, only

only for the Conveniency of meeting his Miſtreſs. This Creature in ſome Time proving very Mercenary, and the Knight unwilling to be impos'd upon, ſhe dogg'd the Lady home, and found out who ſhe was; when once ſhe had got the Secret, ſhe made Sir *Peter* pay what Price ſhe pleas'd for her keeping it; not that his *Vanity* was at all diſpleas'd at the Town's knowing his good Fortune, for he privately boaſted himſelf of it to his Friends, but this Baggage threatned to ſend the Husband and his own Lady News of their Amour.

BEHOLD what a fine Perſon *Rivella* choſe to fool away her Reputation with: I am ſatisfy'd that ſhe was provoked at the Confidence he put in her, and thought her ſelf *piqued* in Honour and Charms to take him from his real Miſtreſs: She was continually bringing in the Lady's Age, in Excuſe of which the Knight often ſaid, *Settee was one of thoſe laſting Beauties that would have Lovers at Fourſcore*; he often admir'd the Delicacy of her Taſte, upon which *Rivella* was ready to burſt with Spleen, becauſe ſhe would not permit her Husband any Favours after ſhe was once engaged with his *Worſhip*, her Conduct and nice Reaſoning forcing the *good plain Man* to be contented with ſeparate Beds.

Sir

Sir *Peter* was however exactly scrupulous in doing Justice to the Lady's Honour; protesting that himself had never had the *Last Favour*, tho' she Lov'd him to Distraction, for fear of Consequences; yet she never scrupled to oblige him so far, as to undress and go even into the naked Bed with him once every Week, where they found a way to please themselves as well as they could.

RIVELLA was wild at being always entertain'd with another Woman's Charms. *Vainlove* used to show her Mrs. *Settee*'s Letters, which were generally as long as a Taylor's Bill, stuff'd with the *faux Brillant*; which yet fed the Knight's Vanity, and almost Intoxicated his Brain. He had found an agreeable Way of entertaining himself near *Rivella*, by talking incessantly of his Mistress; he did not pass a Day without visiting and showing her some of her *Billet-deuxs*. Mean time he was so assiduous near *Rivella*, that Mrs. *Settee* took the Alarm. He always sat behind her in the Box at the Play, led her to her Chair, walk'd with her in the *Park*, introduced her to his Lady's Acquaintance, and omitted no sort of Opportunity to be ever in her Company. *Rivella* put on all her Arts to ingage him effectually, tho' she would never

never hear that she had any such Design; but what else could she mean by a Song which I am going to repeat to you, made upon the Knight's dropping a Letter in her Chamber, writ by his darling Mistress, wherein she complain'd of his Passion for *Rivella?* It began thus; *It is in vain you tell me that I am worship'd and ador'd when you do things so contrary to it*; *Rivella* immediately sent it back to him enclosed with these Verses,

I.

Ah dangerous Swain, tell, tell me no more

Of the blest Nymph you worship and adore;

When thy fill'd Eyes are sparkling at her Name

I raving wish that mine had caus'd the Flame.

II.

If by your Fire for her, you can impart

Diffusive heat to warm another's Heart;

Ah dang'rous Swain! what wou'd the ruin be,

Shou'd you but once persuade you burn for me?

THO' possibly this might be only one of the thoughtless Sallies of *Rivella*'s Wit and Fire, yet it was of the last Consequence to her Reputation: The Knight was perfectly drunk with *Vanity* and *Joy*,

Of RIVELLA.

upon receiving such agreeable Proofs of his Merit: He caused the Words to be set to Notes, and then sung them himself in all Companies where he came: His Flatterers, who were numerous, and did not now want to learn his weak Side, gave him the Title of *the dangerous Swain,* which he prided himself in; till his Mistress grew down right uneasy, and would have him visit *Rivella* no longer. He capitulated, as Reason good, and would be paid his Price for breaking so tender a Friendship, and what so agreeably flatter'd his Vanity, which in short was, as the scandalous Chronicle speaks, that his Mistress should go to Bed to him without Reserve: Either the Weakness of his Constitution, or the Greatness of his Passion, was prejudicial to his Health: He grew proud of the Disorder, and went into a publick Course of Physick, as if it were a worse Matter; finding it extreamly for his Credit, that the Town should believe so well of him (for upon Report of a fair young Lady whom he brought to tread the Stage, that he had pass'd three Days and Nights successively in Bed with her without any Consequence, he was thought rather dangerous to a Woman's Reputation than her Vertue) he would smile and never disabuse his Friends, when they rallied him upon his Disorder: For some Time poor *Rivella*'s Character suffer'd as the Person

Person that had done him this Injury, till seeing him equally assiduous and fond of her in all publick Places, join'd to what the *Operator* discover'd of his pretended Disease; the World found out the Cheat, detesting his Vanity and *Rivella*'s Folly; that cou'd suffer the Conversation of a Wretch so insignificant to her Pleasures, and yet so dangerous to her Reputation.

THIS short liv'd-report did not do *Rivella* any great Prejudice, amongst the Crowd of those who follow'd and flatter'd her with pretended Adoration: She would tell me that her Heart was still untouched, bating a little Concern from her Pride to move old *Vainlove*'s, who so obstinately defended it for another: 'Tis true, she often hazarded Appearances by indulging her natural Vanity, and still continued to do so, tho' perhaps with more Innocency than Discretion; till the Person came, who indeed fix'd her Heart: I am going to shew you a Gentleman of undoubted Merit, accomplish'd both from without and within: His Face was beautiful, so was his Shape, till he grew a little burly. He was bred to Business, as being what you call in *France*, one of the long Robe: His natural Parts prodigious, which were happily join'd by a learned and liberal Education: His Taste delicate, in respect of good Authors;
remark-

remarkable for the Sweetneſs of his Temper, and in ſhort, every way qualified for being Beloved, where ever he ſhould happen to Love.

VALUING my ſelf as I do upon the Reputation of an Impartial Hiſtorian, neither blind to *Rivella*'s Weakneſſes and Misfortunes, as being once her Lover, nor angry and ſevere as remembring I cou'd never be Beloved; I have join'd together the juſt, and the tender, not expatiated with Malice upon her Faults, nor yet blindly overlooking them: If I have happen'd, by repeating her little Vanities, to deſtroy thoſe firſt Inclinations you may have had to eſteem what was valuable in her Compoſition; remember how hard it is in Youth, even for the ſtronger Sex to reſiſt *the ſweet Poyſon of Flattery, and well directed Praiſe or Admiration.*

DURING the ſhort Stay *Rivella* had made in *Hilaria*'s Family, ſhe was become acquainted with the Lord *Crafty*: He had been Ambaſſador in *France*, where his Negotiations are ſaid to have procured as much Advantage to your King, as they did Diſhonour to his own Country. He had a long Head turn'd to Deceit and over-reaching: If a thing were to be done two Ways, he never lov'd the plain, nor
valu'd

valu'd a Point if he could eafily carry it: His Perfon was not at all beholding to Nature, and yet he had poffeffed more fine Women than had the fineft Gentleman, not lefs than twice or thrice becoming his Mafter's Rival. When *Hilaria* was in *France* he found it extreamly convenient for his Affairs to be well with her, as fhe was Miftrefs, and himfelf Ambaffador: For fome Time 'tis fuppofed that he lov'd her out of Inclination, her own Charms being inevitable; but finding fhe was not very regular, he reproach'd her in fuch a Manner, that the haughty *Hilaria* vow'd his Ruin: She would not permit a Subject to take that Freedom fhe would not allow a Monarch, which was, prefcribing Rules for her Conduct: In fhort, her Power was fuch over the King, tho' he was even then in the Arms of a new and younger Miftrefs, and *Hilaria* at fo great a Diftance from him, as to yield to the Plague of her Importunity with which fhe fill'd her Letters. He confented that Lord *Crafty* fhould be recall'd, upon fecret Advice that fhe pretended to have received of his Corruption and Treachery. The Ambaffador did not want either for Friends in *England*, nor in *Hilaria*'s own Family, who gave him very early Advice of what was defign'd againft him: He had the Dexterity to ward the intended Blow, and

turn

turn it upon her that was the Aggreſſor; *Hilaria*'s own Daughter betray'd her to the Ambaſſador: He had corrupted not only her Heart, but ſeduced her from her Duty and Integrity: Her Mother was gone to take the *Bourbon* Waters, leaving this young Lady the Care of her Family, and more immediately of ſuch Letters as a certain Perſon ſhould write to her, full of amorous Raptures for the Favours ſhe had beſtow'd. Theſe fatal Letters, at leaſt ſeveral of them with Anſwers full of Tenderneſs under *Hilaria*'s own Hand, the Ambaſſador proved ſo lucky as to make himſelf Maſter of: He return'd with his *Credentials* to *England* to accuſe *Hilaria* and acquit himſelf: The Miſtreſs was ſummon'd from *France* to juſtify her ill Conduct: What could be ſaid againſt ſuch clear Evidences of her Diſloyalty? 'Tis true, ſhe had to deal with the moſt merciful Prince in the World, and who made the largeſt Allowances for human Frailty, which ſhe ſo far improv'd, as to tell His Majeſty, there was nothing criminal in a Correſpondence deſign'd only for Amuſement, without preſuming to aim at Conſequences; the very *Mode* and *Manner* of Expreſſion in *French* and *Engliſh*, were widely different; that which in one Language carried an Air of extream Gallantry, meant no more than meer Civility in t'other. Whether the Monarch were,

were, or would seem perſuaded, he appear'd ſo, and order'd her to forgive the Ambaſſador; to whom he return'd his Thanks for the Care he had taken of his Glory, very much to *Hilaria*'s Mortification, who was not ſuffer'd to exhibit her Complaint againſt him, which was look'd upon as proceeding only from the Malice and Revenge of a vindictive guilty Woman.

LORD *Crafty* made a very ſucceſsful Embaſſy touching his own Intereſt, tho' he fail'd of bringing the Court altogether into thoſe Meaſures which the *French* King deſired. His Paternal Eſtate was not more than Five thouſand Pound a Year, which he extreamly improv'd, as you may know by the *Rent-Roll*, deliver'd in upon his Son's Marriage, which doubled that Sum ſix Times over, all due to his own Contrivance, wherein he was aſſiſted often by the Ladies, which made him have a very great Opinion of their Management: This Lord us'd to value himſelf upon certain Rules in Policy, of truſting no Perſon with his real Deſigns: What Part he gave any one in his Confidence when they were to negotiate an Affair for him, was in his own Expreſſion but tying 'em by the Leg to a Table, they cou'd not go farther than the Line that held

Of RIVELLA.

held them. He was incapable of Friendship but what made for his Interest, or of Love but for his own proper Pleasures: Nature form'd him a Politician, and Experience made him an Artist in the Trade of Dissimulation; but the best that can be said of those great Parts, which he put to so bad an use, is, that there was a wrong Turn in his Birth, Fortune that caus'd him to be Born the Heir of a good Family mistook his Bent; she had done much better in making him an Attorney, for there was no Point how difficult or knotty soever, but what he could either untie or evade.

HE was married to the Relict of one who had been the richest Merchant in *England*; she brought along with her not only a very large Jointure, but a larger Law-suit, which hit Lord *Crafty*'s Genius; he became much more in Love with That than her Person: Mr. *Double* her Husband was Childless, and had contracted an inviolable Friendship with Baron *Meanwell*, insomuch that they had interchangably made each other their Heir by Deed of Gift. Mr. *Double*'s Affairs call'd him Abroad to the Plantations, which Opportunity his Wife took to revenge her self upon the Baron, for advising her Husband to pull down a very large House and to sell
the

the Ground and Materials to the Builders: This Lady, who was remarkable for her Pride, regretted so fine a Seat, and was resolved to punish Lord *Meanwell* for the Loss of it. She persuaded her Spouse to make a Will in the *Indies*, whereby she relinquish'd one Quarter part of her Joynture, conditionally that Lord *Meanwell*'s Pretensions might be struck out; and young *Double*, who had no Relation to the Merchant but the Name, appointed Heir to the Estate. *During* King *Charles* the First's Troubles, Merchant *Double*'s Father resided at a Seat he had in *Essex* near the Sea-side, he was walking one Evening upon the Strand, regarding several poor half naked, half starv'd Passengers that were getting out of a Ship lately come into the Road; these miserable Wretches were escaped from the *Massacre* in *Ireland*, amongst them was a well look'd Woman with a Boy in her Hand, habited *'en Peasant*: Mr. *Double* ask'd her several Questions, which she answer'd to his Satisfaction, amongst the rest that her Name and her Sons were *Double*, but her Husband had been kill'd by the *Rebels*, which affected him so much, that he order'd her Home to his own House, where she remain'd the rest of her Life: Her Son was made Mr. *Double*'s Gardener; thriving under a flourishing Family he married very well, and also left a Son, a Son, whom old *Double* put into the Army, where he rose to be a Lieutenant Colonel; but did not die rich, leaving a Widow and several Children; the eldest of which, Merchant *Double*'s Lady had picked out, as an Heir worthy to revenge her Quarrel against the Lord *Meanwell:* Her Husband died in the *Indies* not long after he had obliged his Wife in a Point so much to his Dishonour, considering the Deed he had executed in Favour of the Baron: Some Persons who knew the little regard he had for that worthless Brood of the *Doubles*, thought he yielded to his Lady's Importunities only for a quiet Life, thinking he did little more than make her an insignificant Compliment, because two Days before he went to the *Indies*, he had added a *Codicel* which was affix'd to the *Deed*, whereby he for ever incapacitated himself to revoke the said *Deed*, but in the Presence of six Witnesses; two whereof were to be *Prelates* of the Church of *England* ; dying in the *Indies* as he did, whatever Will he could make There, must be defective in that main Article. His Lady return'd with all the Pomp and Splendour of an Eastern Queen; but her Pride working to an excessive Height, soon turn'd her Brain; whereby young *Tim Double* was deprived of a powerful Patroness to carry on those Pretensions she had brought over from the *Indies* in his Favour; and Baron *Meanwell* in all Probability likely to enjoy for himself, and his Heirs for ever, the use Fruit of the foremention'd Deed of Gift.

FORTUNE that loves to mingle her self in all Events, thrust between the *Baron* and his great Hopes the most powerful, most cunning, and most dexterous Adversary that she could possibly have rais'd; it was the Lord *Crafty*, who had swallow'd in his Imagination all *Double*'s Estate: He knew himself blest with a Purse and a Capacity equal to the Work: He therefore bought the Merchant's Widow of her two Women, his own Chaplain married them together; but the Lady being supposed *Non Compos*, it is said one of her Female Directors was, in effect the Bride, lying behind the Pillows, and making proper Answers for the Lunatick; whereby she got to her self the Management of that old Fox, and to the Day of his Death us'd to carry whatever Point she had in Hand, by only threatning to take upon her self, the Title and Quality of his Wife.

LORD *Crafty*, as Reason good, immediately assumed the Management of his Lady's Affairs, and commenced a Suit in young *Tim*'s Name against the Baron; the
Progress

Of RIVELLA.

Progress of that Suit, would make an honest Man for ever detest going to Law; the Point *Crafty* contended for, was to invalidate the *Codicel*, which he attempted to prove spurious. How many *Verdicts* were there given and reversed? What number of Witnesses convicted of Perjury? How much Treasure expended in the Pursuit and the Defence? Our Courts of Judicature rung of nothing else; in the mean time the Cause, was a fat Cause, and the Lawyers contrived how to prolong it whilst none were Gainers but themselves: Baron *Meanwell* almost beggar'd himself; Lord *Crafty* was indeed better circumstanced, but seeing the Delays of the Courts of Justice, and the Tricks of young *Tim Double*; he began to breathe an Air of Accommodation as well as the *Baron*: But *Tim*'s Pretensions being the difficultest Point to be adjusted, they were at a loss how to find a Method by which all things might be settled in that Calm, which the Exigency of both their Affairs seem'd to require.

TIM *Double* prov'd not only a Sot, but the most dissolute, senseless, obstinate Wretch, that a Man could deal with. His Education and natural Parts were both mean, his Temper extravagant and vain; he valu'd himself extreamly upon his Province

vince of Diffimulation, as having practis'd under a very great Master. At the Age of Sixteen he was trapan'd when he was Drunk, to marry the Daughter of a poor *Petty-pan* Merchant; the Girl was Pretty and Ingenious enough; she made him a very good Wife, and often by her Management prevented his being undone by Sharpers, to whom he was naturally addicted: But he hated her, and studied nothing so much as how to get rid of her; tho' to her Face he affected so prodigious a Passion, that he could not breathe without mixing Eyes, pressing and kissing her Hands and Neck; nor would he touch a Bit of Meat but what she cut; nay, he must sit by her at Table, and often eat off of no Plate but hers: This was a fulsom Sight to all who knew he had brought his Marriage into Parliament, where it was likely to have been disannul'd, had not Lord *Crafty* by his underhand Practices prevented it, least *Tim*, becoming a single Man, some rich powerful Family might espouse his Cause, and by Virtue of his Title to so great an Estate, give his Lordship an unexpected Diversion, in the Views he had of gaining it all to himself.

LORD *Crafty* had from time to time supplied him with several large Sums of Money, whereby he pretended to purchase
his

his Title to the whole Estate; but the Point being yet undecided, that was look'd upon no better than *Champarty* and *Maintainance*. *Tim* executed several Deeds, whereby he divested himself of all Pretensions to the Estate, when it should be recover'd; which, when he had done, Lord *Crafty* brought him in a Bill of Threescore Thousand Pounds; some for Monies receiv'd, and the rest for vast Sums expended in the Law-Suit. *Tim* enter'd into Bonds and Judgments, by which he acknowledg'd himself Debtor to my Lord *Crafty*; after which, he was left at Liberty to go where he pleas'd; his Lordship before, never suffering him to stir, but under the Conduct of some Person he could confide in. *Tim*'s Riots were so great, that Lord *Crafty* would no longer supply him with Money; he ran in Debt where-ever he could, till at length he was arrested and forc'd to surrender himself a Prisoner at *Westminster-Hall*, before the *Lord Chief Justice of the Common-pleas*.

IT was perfectly necessary that I should enter into this long Digression, to inform you of the true State of Things, before I give you Knowledge of an Affair, by which *Rivella* was presented with fresh Occasion to renew the Complaint she so justly juftly had againft Fortune, for turning all her Profpects of Good into Evil.

AT that Time *Rivella* liv'd in a pretty Retirement, fome few Miles out of Town, where fhe diverted her felf chiefly with walking and reading. One Day *Califta*, her Sifter Authorefs (with whofe Story I may hereafter entertain you, as well as with the other writing Ladies of our Age) came, as ufual, to make her a Vifit; fhe told her that *Cleander*, a Friend of hers, one of the moft accomplifh'd Perfons living, was in Cuftody of a *Serjeant of Arms* for fome Misdemeanours, which were nothing in themfelves, but as he had been of Council on Lord *Crafty*'s Side, againft Lord *Meanwell*, and was fuppos'd to have had the chief Conduct of the laft Trial, Matters were like to be partially carried, becaufe *Ofwald* (poor *Rivella*'s Kinfman and Husband, tho' fhe always hated his being call'd fo) was appointed Chairman of the Committee order'd to examine *Cleander*; and *Ofwald* being long known a Champion for Lord *Meanwell*, in refpect of his Caufe, it was very juftly fear'd, that he would joyn Revenge and Retaliation to his own native Temper of Choler and Fury, by which Means *Cleander* was to expect very fevere Ufage, if not a worfe Misfortune.

TO conclude; after *Califta* had rais'd *Rivella*'s Pity, Wonder, and Curiosity, for the Merit, Beauty, and Innocence of the Gentleman under Prosecution; she proposed a real Advantage to her self, if she could influence her Kinsman to stand neuter in the Cause; or if that was not to be expected, that she would so far ingage him, that he should keep away on the Day which was appointed for *Cleander*'s Examination.

RIVELLA was always inclin'd to assist the Wretched; neither did she believe it Prudence to neglect her own Interest, when she found it meritorious to persue it: She told *Califta*, that being only her Friend was enough to ingage her to endeavour at serving this *Cleander* whoever he were; but that since she had taken Care to add Interest to Friendship, which were Motives her Circumstances were no way qualified to refuse, she was resolved upon that double Consideration, to attempt doing whatever was in her Power for both their Services; but because she was not willing to embark without some Prospect of a fortunate Voyage, she desired to speak with *Cleander* in Person, as well to inform her self of the Merits of the Cause, as to be acquainted with a Gentleman of whom she had given so advantagious a Description.

CALISTA blush'd at the Proposal, which *Rivella* observing, immediately ask'd her, if he were her Lover, which would be enough to ingage her to serve him without any other Motive; and thereupon said, that she would be contented to take Minutes from *Califta* only, without concerning her self any further about being acquainted with *Cleander*.

CALISTA who was the most of a *Prude* in her outward Professions, and the least of it in her inward Practice, unless you'll think it no *Prudery* to allow Freedoms with the Air of Restraint; ask'd *Rivella* with a scornful Smile, What it was she meant? *Cleander* was a married Man, and as such, out of any Capacity to engage her secret Service; her Friendship was meerly with his Wife, and as such if she would assist him, she should be oblig'd to her for her Trouble. *Rivella* who hates Dissimulation, especially amongst Friends, was resolved to pique *Califta* for her Insincerity, and therefore said, since it was so; she insisted upon seeing and informing her self from *Cleander*'s own Mouth, or else she would not ingage in the Business.

THE next Day *Cleander* sent a Gentleman to wait upon *Rivella*, and beg her Interest in his Service, together with the Promise and Assurance of a certain Sum of Money if she should succeed.

THESE Preliminaries settled, the Day after *Cleander* sent the same Person (who happen'd to be a sort of an insignificant Gentleman, acquainted long since both with *Rivella* and himself) in a Chariot, with an unknown Livery to bring her to Town, and even to the *Serjeant at Arms*'s House, where *Cleander* was at that time confin'd.

RIVELLA had formed to her self what it was going to speak to a Man of Business in Private, that she must at least wait till the Croud were dismiss'd, and therefore took a Book in her Pocket, that she might entertain her self with reading whilst she waited for Audience: She chose the Duke *de Rochfoucaut*'s Moral Reflections; she had not attended long, before *Cleander* came to Wait on her, tho' but for two or three Moments till he could dismiss his Company, praying her to be easy till he might have the Honour to return; during this short Compliment, *Rivella* had thrown her Book upon the Table, *Cleander* whilst he was speaking took it up, as not heeding

heeding what he did, and departed the Room with the Book in his Hand: Who that has ever dipp'd into those Reflections, does not know that there is not a Line there, but what excites your Curiosity, and is worth being eternally admired and remembred? *Cleander* had never met with it before: He form'd an Idea from that Book of the Genius of the Lady, who chose it for her Entertainment, and tho' he had but an indifferent Opinion hitherto of Woman's Conversation, he believ'd *Rivella* must have a good Taste from the Company she kept. He found an Opportunity of confirming himself, before he parted, in *Rivella*'s Sense, and Capacity for Business as well as Pleasure; which were agreeably mingled at Supper, none but those two Gentlemen and *Rivella* being present. Behold the beginning of a Friendship which endured for several Years even to *Cleander*'s Death. He was married Young, but as yet knew not what it was to Love: His Studies and Application to Business, together with the Desire of making himself great in the World, had employ'd all his Hours; Neither did his Youth and Vigour stand in need of Diversions to relieve his Mind; he was civil to his Lady, meant very well for her Children, and did not then dream there was any thing in her Person defective to his Happiness, that was in

the

Of RIVELLA

the Power of any other of that Sex to beſtow.

EARLY in the Morning *Rivella* went to *Weſtminſter-Hall*, ſhe took up her Poſt at the *Bookſellers-Shop*, by the Foot of thoſe Stairs which go up to the Parliament-houſe: She had not waited long but ſhe ſaw her Kinſman; he was cover'd with Bluſhes and Confuſion, not imagining what Buſineſs ſhe had there, unleſs to expoſe him; he had not even ſeen her Face in ſome Years nor ſhe his, having ſought nothing ſo much as to avoid one another.

RIVELLA advanced to ſpeak with him, he bluſh'd more and more, ſeveral Members coming by to go to the Houſe, and obſerving him with a Lady in his Hand, he thought it was beſt to take her from that publick Place, and therefore led her the back Way out of the *Hall*, call'd a Coach put her in it, and afterwards got in himſelf without having Power to ask her what Buſineſs brought her to enquire after him in a Place ſo improper for Converſation, at the ſame Time ordering the Coachman to drive out of Town.

THUS was that important Affair neglected, they choſe another *Chairman* for the *Committee*, which ſat that Morning: *Cleander* was acquitted, with the uſual Reprimand,

primand, and order'd to be set at Liberty, very much to the Regret of *Oswald* when he came coolly to consider how scandalously he had abandon'd an Affair of that Importance, and which Lord *Meanwell* had left wholly to his Management.

BEFORE *Rivella* parted with her Spouse, she told him, what was her design'd Request, and the Motive. He seem'd very well pleas'd that nothing but Interest had engag'd her: He bid her be sure to cultivate a Friendship with *Cleander*, who would doubtless come to return his Thanks for the Service she had done him; recommending to her at the same Time, *First*, not to receive the Money which had been promised her, because there were better Views, and which would be of more Importance to her Fortune; and *Secondly*, to leave her House in the Country for some Time, to come and take Lodgings in *London*, where he would wait upon her to direct her in the Management of some great Affair.

BEHOLD *Rivella* in a new Scene, that of Business; in which however Love took Care to save all his own Immunities: He bespoke the most considerable Place for *Cleander*, who often visited her with a Pleasure new and surprizing to his hitherto to insensible Breast: I was lately come to Town: *Rivella*'s Conversation always made Part of my Pleasure, if not my Happiness; so that whenever she allow'd me that Favour, I never omitted waiting on her: Some Presentiment told me this agreeable Gentleman would certainly succeed: I saw his Eyes always fix'd on her with unspeakable Delight, whilst hers languish'd him some Returns: He approv'd rather than applauded what she said, but would always shift Places, till he got one next her, omitting no Opportunity to touch her Hand, when he could do it without any seeming Design: I told her she had made a Conquest; and one that she ought to value her self upon; for *Cleander* was assuredly a Man of Worth as well as Beauty: She laugh'd, and said he was so awkard, and so unfashion'd as to love; that if he did bear her any great good Will, she was sure he neither durst, nor knew how to tell it her: I perceiv'd the Pleasure she took in speaking of him: Wherefore I came in with my old Way of Caution and Advice, bidding her have a Care: One Affair with a married Man did a Woman's Reputation more Harm than with Six others: Wives were with reason so implacable, so invenom'd against those who supplanted them, that they never forbore to revenge themselves at the Expence of of their Rival's Credit; for if nothing else ensu'd, a total Deprivation of the World's Esteem, was sure to be the Consequence of an injur'd Wife's Resentment: *Cleander* was too handsom a Man to be lost with any Patience; his Wife was much older than himself, and much a Termagant, therefore nothing but Fire and Fury could be expected from such a Domestick Evil: The Deprivation of a charming Husband's Heart, being capable to rouse the most insensible: *Rivella* laugh'd, and thank'd me for my Advice, but how she profited by it a very little Time will shew us.

HER Kinsman (I chuse to call him so, rather than by that hateful Name her Husband) caress'd her with the utmost Blandishments; he told her it was now in her own Power to redeem all the Mismanagement they had both been guilty of in respect of her Fortune: *Cleander* was the Person that could do Miracles in Point of Accommodation between Lord *Crafty* and Baron *Meanwell*: He empower'd her to make him very advantagious Offers, if he would but use his Interest towards composing that Affair. She sounded *Cleander* upon that Head: He answer'd her as a Person who could refuse nothing to a Woman he lov'd, but at the same Time told her they were all mistaken; he had

not

Of RIVELLA.

not any Part of Lord *Crafty*'s Confidence which he was now very glad of, becaufe he muft either difoblige her, or, which was a worfe Evil, betray my Lord: Nay more, his Lordfhip had been wanting in doing him little Services during his Confinement, which he would nor eafily forgive; that true indeed he had been of *Council* for him in the laft Trial; but not *trufted*; tho' that very Sufpicion had drawn upon him Lord *Meanwell*'s Difpleafure, and *Ofwald*'s Perfecution, notwithftanding which, Lord *Crafty* had fail'd of Generofity enough to ftand by him, perhaps not efteeming him of fufficient Confequence to his Service: *Rivella* reported this back to her *Principal*; he would not believe *Cleander*, which made her likewife diftruft his Integrity; he never came to vifit her, but fhe always teiz'd him with thefe Words, *You can oblige me! you can retrieve my broken Fortune! you can give Peace to* Weftminfter-Hall, *between thofe mighty Potentates that have fo long divided it! and you refufe to do it! did I ferve you with fuch an Ill-will, or by halves? Ceafe profeffing your Gratitude and Friendfhip to me when it rifes no higher than common Effects; you had better never vifit, than difoblige me.* Cleander was quite vanquifh'd by her Reproaches and Importunity; the Evil was in his
L   Heart,

Heart, he could not refrain seeing her, and took this Opportunity to declare himself, by telling her his Opinion, was, *that no Lover either could, or ought to refuse what was ask'd him by the Person he lov'd.* In short, he gave her to understand, that he had not any Obligation to Lord *Crafty*, and he was very glad of it, but that he thought the Baron's Way did not lie towards an Accommodation with that Lord, but with Mr. *Timothy Double*, because if Matters were agreed between them two, and the *Deed* and the *Will* joyn'd, what had Lord *Crafty* to do in it any further than to expect to find his Wife's Jointure well paid: Double *is a Prisoner*, said *Cleander, where I command*; *if you*, Madam, *were secur'd, so that our Interest could become mutual, and we not make our selves the* Baron's, *or your* Kinsman's *Tools, I don't find there would be any great Difficulty in bringing this Matter to bear.*

RIVELLA immediately gave Part of her Secret to her Cousin, and he to the *Baron*; they could not help wondring at their own Blindness which had till then miss'd so obvious a Mark. The *Baron* admitted *Cleander*'s Genius for Business, and order'd *Rivella* to meet his Lordship at a Third Place, there to take his Instructions:

ons: He began with assuring her of his entire Confidence in her Honour and Capacity, bidding her make it *Cleander*'s Interest to conclude this Project of Reconciliation, for which when it was accomplish'd they should have between them Eight Thousand Pounds paid down upon the Nail; it was her Business, either to come in for half, or to make what Terms she could with *Cleander*; that in the mean Time *Tim Double* should be introduc'd to her Lodgings, where they would have her entertain and caress him to all the Height of his own extravagant Humour: In a few Days they should be able to see whether the Project would bear, which if it did not, *Rivella* should have a Present of an Hundred Guineas, to defray what Expence she might be at, and over and above his Lordship's Acknowledgment and Protection as long as he liv'd. *Cleander*, to oblige *Rivella*, agreed to these Proposals, because he could not refuse what she so earnestly insisted on; but he bid her remember it was only to please her, not thro' any great Prospect he had of advantaging himself, because the Persons they had to deal with, he fear'd, had not all the Honour that was requir'd in such an Affair, where much more was to be left to the *Bona Fide* than to any Security, that could, as Matters stood,

stood, be made obligatory or binding in Law.

THUS was *Timothy Double* introduc'd to *Rivella*'s Appartment; but before he could make his Appearance there, poor *Cleander* was forc'd to accouter him at his own Coft; he was horribly out of Humour becaufe he was very much out of Repair. Therefore he fent him his Taylor, of whom *Tim* immediately befpoke Two Suits that came to more than Sixfcore Pound, full of Gold and Silver. The Perriwigmaker furnifh'd him upon *Cleander*'s Credit, with two Perriwigs upwards of Thirty Guineas apiece: Lace and Linnen made another improving Article; fo that before *Cleander* durft ask him a Queftion, he was dipp'd above Three Hundred Pound for his Service, without putting one Piece into his Pocket: He would not truft him with ready Money, left he fhould elope, and fall again into fome of the Hands of his old Comrades the Sharpers. *Cleander* did not fail to hint to *Rivella* the Expence he had been at to pleafe her Humour; at the fame Time making her obferve Lord *Meanwell*'s Parfimony, that would venture no more than an Hundred Guineas, and that not paid down, to gain fo vaft an Advantage to himfelf as an Accommodation with *Tim*, asking her with a Smile, how one of her great Soul, could so earnestly engage her Cares and Interest for the Service of him, who had so little a Soul?

TIM stuck full of Gold and Silver Lace, made a tolerable Figure, he was neither ugly nor conceited; his Habit having so much of the fine Gentleman, the worst of it was, his Conversation did not well agree with his Dress; but he had been long enough with Lord *Crafty* to learn an outward Civility, his Behaviour was seemingly modest and full of Bows; *Cleander* brought him to *Rivella*, as an injur'd Gentleman, who had been ruin'd by that Lord's Refinements: *Tim* presently recounted several pleasant Acts of Management, which would make no ill Figure in secret History. *Cleander* was obliged to endure this Booby for several Days, to drink with him, nay, to sleep with him, till he had gotten into his Confidence; in all that Time never naming Lord *Meanwell*'s Name; that Task was left to *Rivella*, of whose good Sense and Honour he gave *Tim* a very advantagious Character: They used generally to Dine with her, she did Pennance enough, being obliged to deny her self to all other Company, and to lengthen out Dinner till it came to Supper Time, from whence *Tim* must always go to

the

the Tavern before he went to Bed. Miserable *Cleander* kept him Company, for fear he should get some of his old Gang, who were Spies gain'd by Lord *Crafty*: In Conclusion he began to talk freely with *Rivella* by way of unlading his Grievances, the Wretchedness of his Circumstances; great Debts and Incumbrance with Lord *Crafty*, did not make him half so uneasy as the Difficulty of being rid of his Wife: Tho' he was sure he could still be divorced from her, if he had any Friend to stand by him, who would be kind enough to assist him with his Purse: This naturally introduced Lord *Meanwell*, of whose Vertues *Rivella* made a pompous Dissertation, which much surprized *Tim* who had been used to hear the *Baron* treated as the greatest *Fourb* in Nature: The first thing instill'd into him was the Forgery of the Clause, which had been annexed to old *Double*'s Deed. *Rivella* endeavour'd to set him right as to that suspicious Circumstance, and with much more ease and Justice display'd Lord *Crafty* in his political Capacity; *Tim* could help her in her Task, and did not scruple to give her many Instances relating to himself, particularly one Night when Lord *Crafty* got *Tim* behind a Table with Deeds and Conveyances before him, to which end he had kept him close up for several Days, *Tim*'s Nose fell a Bleeding, he rose to fetch a Hand-

Handkerchief, my Lord would not let him go but presented him his own, which being quickly wet, the Lawyer and his Witnesses supplied him with theirs; in Conclusion they would have suffer'd him to bleed to Death, rather than stir till he had sign'd and seal'd, according to his Lordship's own Heart's Desire.

BY these Practices *Tim* was ruin'd to all Intents and Purposes and condemn'd to perish in Prison, without he could relieve himself by some other Method than had yet been taken. He had cost *Cleander* just Five hundred Pound when *Rivella* proposed to him an Accommodation with Lord *Meanwell*, in which the young Man was at first very sincere: But here the Parcimony of that Lord, or the Folly of his Manager *Oswald* spoil'd all; *Rivella* was of *Tim*'s side, and, Reason good, strove to make as advantagious a Bargain for him as she could; nothing would serve *Tim* but to be made a Lord, he had all the Time of *Crafty*'s Management been flatter'd with a much greater Title when the Estate shou'd be once recovered: That which stuck hardest with *Tim*, was a Point which Lord *Meanwell* strenuously insisted upon, nay, would do nothing without, *viz*. parting with the superbious chief Seat of the *Doubles*, which the *Baron* wanted to settle upon

upon his second Son whom he lov'd extreamly. *Tim* was told that as Matters stood, it was infinitely too large for any Expence he could ever hope to make, but in Exchange he should have the Lord *Meanwell*'s own House, with all the Furniture, which was a much more modern Structure, and where he constantly resided when he was in Town, and with it, the House-keeper's Place belonging to one of the King's Palaces where *Tim* would have occasion to commence Courtier, a Province he excessively long'd for, besides frequent Opportunities to oblige the Maids of Honour in the Choice of their Lodging, which weigh'd very much with *Tim*'s amorous Temper: He desired to view the Inside of the House, to know whether it was a Habitation fit for a Man of so great a Soul; this was a difficult Point, which yet he insisted on so far, that he would treat no further unless he lik'd the House, that which he was to resign in Lieu of it, being the Idol of his Fancy, tho' no way suitable to any but an overgrown Estate: The *Baron* very well knew Lord *Crafty* had Spies in his Family who would soon carry the Report to him of *Tim Double*'s being to visit his House, which must certainly ruin the whole Treaty; they were at their Wits end to get him to pass over that Circumstance, but *Tim* was obstinate and would not be persuaded;

at

Of RIVELLA

at length, Women being good at Invention, *Rivella* found a Method how to gratify *Tim*'s Curiosity, and in a Way which hit his Vein, having a great Inclination to be dabling with Politicks and Intrigues; the next *Sunday* the *Baron* and all his Family were purposely to dine abroad, Leave shou'd be given to the Servants to do what they would with themselves, which, if not given them, they are apt enough to take when their Attendance is not required at home: His Chaplain he could so far confide in, as to tell him two Clergymen from the *University* had a Curiosity to see the House *incognito*, which for certain Reasons he desired him to show: A Servant whom the *Baron* had long trusted was to let in the *Oxonians*, and introduce them to the Chaplain.

TWO Clergymen's Habits were sent to *Rivella*'s Lodgings, where the Pious Gentlemen were to take Orders; she had sent the Landlady and all the Family to divert themselves at her Country House, and left no Soul with her self but an under Servant, whom she dispatch'd to Church: It fell a Raining with great Violence for the rest of the Day; the Sparks came after Dinner, and were soon metamorphosed into spruce *Clergymen: Tim* had a *French* Brocade Vest under his Habit which nevertheless durst not appear ; the Difficulty of getting a Coach on *Sundays*, and especially in rainy Weather, made them keep theirs: *Tim* had contracted such an ill Habit of Swearing, that he could neither leave it off nor knew when he did it ; *Rivella* call'd the Coachman in, and told him the Persons he brought thither had sent him his Money, having no occasion to go farther : But there were two Ministers above that wanted a Coach, the Fellow brush'd up his Seats, and in they got, *Cleander* gave him Directions where to go, which he not taking readily, *Tim* fell a swearing at him for a Blockhead and a Dunce; the Man stared, got up nimbly into his Coach-box, snapt his Whip, and swore as loud as *Tim* had done, that he never saw such *Pasons* in his Life.

ALL things were display'd to the best Advantage at Lord *Meanwell*'s ; *Tim* liked it well enough when his Thoughts had no Return of that Glorious Seat in the Country, which often cost him many a Pang to forgo; but to comfort himself, he would needs see the Cellars, the Chaplain waited on him down, and civilly offer'd him his Choice, either of *Champaign* or *Burgundy* ; *Tim* liked both, and in he sat for it, *Cleander* winked at him in vain, jogg'd his Knee, no Notice took honest *Tim*,
the

the Glass went about, the Chaplain was disposed to stare, seeing him swallow down the Liquor so greedily; at length, *Cleander* told *Tim* in his Ear, it was necessary they should be gone before Church was done: *Tim* answer'd aloud, that might be, But where was there so good *Burgundy* to be had after Church? *Cleander* was at his Wits end at the Incivility of the Brute; *Tim* laid about him, as if all the Wine in the Cellar was his own, because the House and Furniture were to be so if he pleas'd. *Cleander* grew wild to get him away, and told him, with that Reverend Gentleman's leave, they would take some Bottles with them in the Coach to drink when they came home. The Chaplain's Commission did not extend so far, his Lord was a good Husband of his Wines, and yet he knew not how to refuse; in short, he yielded that they should have half a dozen Bottles: But when they came to the Gate the Coachman was gone unpaid; probably the Fellow knew they were the same Persons he had carried before in a Lay-Habit, and did not know what to make of them, yet not daring to mutter, seeing them go into such a House: *Tim* was half bouzy, and without any Respect to his Cloth, with a Bottle in each Hand, stood in the Street calling *Coach! Coach!* the Rain still continuing no Coach came; the

Chaplain and *Cleander*, likewise with each their two Bottles in Hand, were something abashed, and did not call *Coach! Coach!* so loud as did *pot valiant Tim*; at length, the Expedient was found of sending the *Baron*'s Servant for two Chairs: *Tim* would have all the six Bottles along with him in his own Chair, they were carried back again to *Rivella*'s, where they unrob'd and ended this troublesom Adventure.

TIM having at length agreed to an Exchange of Houses, being persuaded to allow in Point of Grandeur for the difference of Town and Country, the Treaty went on; he was promised to be relieved from all his Ingagements to Lord *Crafty*. He demanded two thousand Pounds a Year to be settled upon him and his Heirs for ever; to be assisted in his Divorce, and if that could be effected, that he might have leave to Court one of the *Baron*'s Daughters; to receive ten Thousand Pounds in ready Money, and be made a Lord; this last Article was readily complied with, a Patent for a *Barony* valu'd at ten Thousand Pound being found in the Family, granted by the late King for Services done, the other two Articles they thought too large, and therefore offer'd but one Thousand Pound a Year, and six in Money.

Of RIVELLA.

LORD *Meanwell*'s Oversight lay in not fixing *Tim*'s inconstant Temper whilst he might have done it; the Squire quickly wanted a Change of Place, Circumstances and Diversion: The Baron ought to have clos'd with *Tim*'s Terms, when he could have had them, and not lost irrecoverable Time in striving to beat down the Market, tho' he confess'd it was cheap, and what he would gladly give rather than go without: Besides, his worthless *Plenipo*, *Oswald*, who pretended to his Lordship that he served for nought, when he saw Matters were just beginning to bear, told *Rivella* that he understood *Cleander* had consented that she should divide with him the Eight Thousand Pound, which himself very unworthily expected to divide with her. He would have Two Thousand for his own Use, and the other Two Thousand settled after her Death, upon a Son which had been the Product of their Marriage.

RIVELLA answer'd him, that provided the Baron were acquainted with these Conditions, she would agree with them, how remote soever from what had been first promised her; but if otherwise, she would not be any longer impos'd upon by *Oswald*'s Pretences: This caus'd bad
Blood

Blood between them; he began to be jealous of *Tim*, without suspecting *Cleander*: He put himself into Passions and Disgusts, and wore out the Time in Complaints and Expostulations, yet took Part of all those fine Dinners that were every Day seen at *Rivella*'s; for which, when she desir'd him to represent to the Baron the Expence she was unavoidably put to, he once brought her the paultry Sum of Three Pound, which, as she said, would not furnish one *Desert*; and this was all the Money ever tender'd her from the *Baron* in that Affair, tho' she reasonably presum'd his Lordship, according to his own Proposal, had trusted larger Sums for her Use into the Hands of his Treasurer *Oswald*.

BUT whilst *Oswald* was contriving how to reduce *Tim*'s Demands, secure Two Thousand Pound to himself without the Baron's Knowledge, and get the other Two Thousand Pound settled in reversion upon his Son, an unforeseen, and as one should think an inconsiderable Accident, let all of them see the Vanity of pretending to divide the Spoil before the Prey was secur'd.

THERE was a Girl about Seventeen or Eighteen, nam'd *Bella*, who sometimes frequented the Play-house, but as yet could get no Salary; for a Year or Two together she us'd to come to *Rivella*'s when she
was

was in Town, to beg her to speak to the *Managers*, that she might be receiv'd into Pay: She was a poor Woman's Daughter in the Neighbourhood, which ingaged *Rivella* to promise her what little Interest she had: *Bella* us'd sometimes to come to Dinner there, as she did at other Places, offering her Service in making up Heads, and those little Offices wherein the Girl was tolerably handy: When there was no Company, *Rivella* had sometimes the Goodness to make her sit down at the Table with her, otherwise she us'd to be glad to get a Meals Meat with Mrs. *Flippanta*, *Rivella*'s Woman: That Wench, was perfectly *Mercurial*, and had the greatest Propensity to Intrigue, and bringing People together; tho' her Lady was not then acquainted with her Talent, no more than her other Qualification of Dissimulation; for she was perfectly demure before her Mistress: *Bell* was greatly in her Favour, because she us'd at spare Times to entertain her with Scraps of Plays and amorous Speeches in Heroicks: The Landlady and another Woman who lodg'd in the House where *Rivella* lodg'd, were fond of the same Amusement: *Bell* was much oftner there than *Rivella* knew, and when she was abroad, the Wench was always repeating in a Theatrical Tone and Manner.

LORD

LORD *Meanwell's* Phlegm, or Irrefolution, made the Treaty hang long, together with *Ofwald's* very ill Humour about the Four Thousand Pounds, which he had swallow'd in his Imaginations, joyn'd to his pretended Jealousy of *Tim*, so that *Rivella* was grown weary, and glad to go abroad for a little Relief, leaving the House to *Tim* and *Ofwald* to drink in; as for *Cleander*, I presume he was but seldom there; when *Rivella* was not, Mrs. *Flippanta* made a Figure in her Lady's Absence, and *Bella* by this Means came to be seen by *Tim*; he fell in Love with her according to his Way of loving: The Girl had a round Face, not well made, large dull Eyes, but she was young, and well enough complexion'd, tho' she wanted Air, and had a Defect in her Speech, which were two Things they objected against as to her coming into the Play-House. *Tim* bribed *Flippanta* to get the Girl's Company in her Lady's Absence, as he would have done for any Girl that came in his Way. They were grown very well acquainted, before *Tim* told the News of his growing Flame to *Cleander*; which he spoke of as a Thing indispensibly necessary to his Happiness: *Tim* fancied himself some mighty considerable Person, he had three very great Affairs upon his Hands, to end with my Lord *Meanwell*, get rid of his Wife, and poffefs himfelf of *Bell*'s Favours: *Cleander* told *Rivella* what a Scrape they were brought into, and conjur'd her not to oppofe him; for if *Tim* was crofs'd in his Humour, all was at an End: He was already dipp'd feveral Hundred Pounds; for that fine 'Squire, 'tis fuppos'd, could not be kept all this Time without Money in his Pocket, and a great deal too. The Affair had been fo long depending, that his Wife found out his Haunt at *Rivella*'s, of which fhe immediately gave Notice to Lord *Crafty*: She was fix'd immoveably to his Lordfhip's Service, notwithftanding her Husband's Intereft, which *Tim* had honeftly told *Cleander* in the Beginning, and therefore begg'd he might remain conceal'd from his Wife till all was concluded with the Baron: Lord *Crafty* knew fo much of *Rivella*'s Temper, that fhe would not have endur'd fuch a Booby as *Tim*, and have made great Expence upon him without better Views: He heard of *Tim*'s Bravery, and what Airs he gave himfelf: Lord *Crafty* had never been fo defective in any Point of Policy as in abandoning of *Tim*; it muft coft him confiderable to retrieve that falfe Step: It was no hard Matter to find his Lodging by dogging him from *Rivella*'s Houfe, which when once done, he sent a Person to him, call'd old *Simon*, who had long been Lord *Crafty*'s Creature, and by humouring *Tim* in his Vices and Vanities, had gain'd an absolute Ascendant over him; but when *Tim* grew poor and no longer of Consequence to Lord *Crafty*, Mr. *Simon* forsook him with the rest, yet soon regain'd his former Station by Flattery; and finding the Place of a Favourite vacant, he reassum'd it as formerly. *Tim* ask'd *Cleander* to intercede with *Rivella* that Mr. *Simon* might be permitted to make one of the Company: *Rivella* told them they were undone from that Minute, he was a Creature of my Lord *Crafty*'s and the whole Design would certainly come to nothing: *Tim* assur'd *Cleander* that *Simon* was a Convert and hated my Lord's ill Usage of him as much as they did: *Rivella* knew *Tim*'s Tallent at Dissembling, which he openly valu'd himself upon, and therefore did not much regard what he said; she sent to the *Baron* to give him Notice of this Accident: Then his Lordship's and *Oswald* began to put themselves upon the Frett; *Tim* had sometime since sunk his Pretensions, of two Thousand to fifteen Hundred Pounds a Year, and was come to close with their own offer of six Thousand Pound in Money, which these shallow, or greedy Politicians finding, thought to sink him further, and in that

that View kept the Affair so long in hand that it got Wind; but then Lord *Meanwell* began to bestir himself too late, he order'd *Rivella* to tell the Squire, that he did agree to all his Demands, and was accordingly seeing the Writings perfected; in the mean Time, the Articles were drawing up for *Tim* to sign, upon which, he was to receive eight Hundred Pound overplus for his present Necessities: *Simon* had leave given to make one at *Rivella*'s, and she had Orders to assure him of a Present of five Hundred Pound for his own Occasions.

MEAN Time, *Tim*'s Flame for *Bella* daily increas'd, *Rivella* call'd her to her, and bid her keep away from her House; for she would not charge her self with the Consequences, Squire *Tim* being a married Man: The Girl did not scruple to tell her, that her Design of going to the Playhouse was in hopes of finding some body to keep her, she had often seen in the Dressing Room, what great Respect Mrs. *Barry* and the rest, used to pay to Mrs. *Alyfe* when she used to come thither, and how fine they all liv'd, which she was sure they cou'd not do upon their Pay. *Rivella* was amaz'd at her Confidence, which she thought no way suitable to a Maid: She then spoke to *Tim* to give over the Pursuit, since that Girl could not possibly be of any Consequence to a Man like him, and to ruin her, would be an eternal Reproach to the whole Company; *Tim* swore he would marry her to morrow, or as soon as he was divorced, and old *Simon* thought this a very good Handle, he made his Court in the Squire's name more artfully to the Girl. He assured her that *Rivella* was her mortal Enemy, and envied her least she should come to be greater than herself: For *Tim* had indeed told *Rivella*, as I said before, that if he could be divorced he would marry *Bella*; this gain'd his Point with the Girl: She assumed very haughty Airs towards *Rivella*, and very tender ones towards *Tim*: Old *Simon* had likewise succeeded his Court to *Flippanta*, by making believe he was smitten with her Beauty: Poor decay'd *Flip* was proud of a Conquest, and readily entered into a Confederacy against her Mistress: To conclude, *Bella* was become the Head of the Company, neither durst *Rivella* contradict her. She thought some small Time longer would put an end to her Suffering, and betray'd as little Uneasiness as possible. *Simon* persuaded *Tim* that he had no other way to preserve *Bella*'s Favour, but by breaking that dishonourable Treaty he had been drawn into with the Lord *Meanwell*; *Bella* assured him of the same thing: *Simon* told him, that Lord *Crafty* heartily repented the Neglect

Of RIVELLA.

glect had been shown whilst his Lordship was in the Country, and to make appear that he was sincere, offer'd to give him up all his Ingagements, and to prosecute the Suit against the *Baron*, till he had put him in Possession of the whole Estate. *Tim* did not know which Part to chuse, when he was with *Bell* and *Sim*, he was Theirs, when he was with *Cleander* and *Rivella* he was for Them; at length, the long look'd for Hour came, when he was to sign the Articles and receive his eight Hundred Pounds Bounty Money: The *Baron* would needs have him come alone to the Tavern where they were to meet, that so the Act might look voluntary; but, the Difficulty was how to get him there; they durst not so much as tell him, least he should give Part of the Intelligence to Mr. *Simon*; in short, it was left to *Rivella*'s Management, she took him out in a Coach with her to the appointed Place, upon Pretence of meeting a Gentleman who had a Mind to part with a Diamond Buckle for his Hat, and if *Tim* lik'd it, he might become a Proprietor in the Buckle, and have six Month's Credit given him; this was something that hit the *Squire*'s Vanity; but as they were going thither, *Rivella* told him the real Design; but that since the utmost Secrefy was necessary, she had used that Artifice to prevent Mr. *Simon*, and consequently

quently Lord *Crafty* from knowing his good Fortune till it was beyond their Power to prevent: She said, that faithful *Cleander* attended with the Lord *Meanwell*'s Lawyer, who for his own Honour, as well as out of Respect and friendship for *Tim*, would take care to have all possible Justice done him in an Affair that was going to make such a Noise in the World: To be short, *Rivella* fortified him so well that he promised to go in and perform what he had covenanted; she set him down two Doors, short of the Tavern, he kiss'd her Hand with an Air entirely satisfied, and told her she shou'd always command that Fortune, which she had been so good to procure for him; and that the next Day at Dinner, he would do himself the Honour to wait upon her to pay his Acknowledgments more at large: Thus was that great Affair dispatched; and the eighth Day after appointed for executing the Deeds, and putting the Squire in Possession of what Estate and Money had been stipulated for him.

OLD *Simon* revell'd with the Money *Tim* brought home, who had never the Honesty to repay *Cleander* the least Part of what he had borrow'd of him; as to *Rivella*'s Expences, they were come to a Sum so much beyond what the *Baron* had promis'd her, in case that Affair did not succeed,

Of RIVELLA.

succeed, that she never demanded any Money from him; throwing *at all*, as in a desperate Game; where nothing less can repair the former Loss.

THE eighth Day did come; the Lord and his Agent, the Deeds and the Lawyers were ready; but not the Squire: Old *Simon* and Mr. *Timothy*, Madam *Bell* and *Mademoiselle Flippanta* silently dislodged without Beat of Drum, and left *Cleander* and *Rivella* to repent of their grand expensive Negotiation; by which in the end, no Persons happened to be Gainers, but the Lord *Crafty* and Mr. *Simon*.

I WILL not tire you with many more Particulars: *Tim* was infatuated by *Bell*'s Persuasions who now lodged with him as his Lady, but *incog*, for Fear of the *Baron* and *Cleander:* Lord *Crafty* let them spend together the Money *Tim* had so basely acquired, and then sent him away to *Flanders* under *Sim*'s Conduct, who took care to confine him to a House they had taken, not suffering him to converse with any Company, but three or four Rakes that they had gotten purposely to drink with him from Morning till Night, keeping him perpetually fluster'd, least his cooler Sense should make him consider what he had done, and put him upon stealing away from

from them to return back into *England*, there to perform Articles with the Lord *Meanwell*. Treacherous *Bell* was likewife over-reach'd, fhe was put for fometime to Penfion by a feign'd Name at a poor Woman's Houfe in an obfcure Part of the Town, with daily Promifes of being fent into *Flanders* to her Beloved, who had ftipulated with Lord *Crafty*'s Agent that fhe fhould follow him; telling *Rivella* and others that he was married to her, which whether true or falfe fignified little, fince *Bell* very well knew, unlefs he could make his former Marriage null, *Tim* was in no Capacity to marry again.

HERE that infignificant treacherous Creature grew Poor and was forgotten; for when *Bell* no longer ferved their Ends, Lord *Crafty* and his *Managers* remembred her no more than if fhe never had been born; a very quick Return for her Perfidy, Folly and Ingratitude; had fhe not feduced *Tim Double* from his Engagements, *Cleander* would have taken care of her Interefts fo far (fince her higheft Ambition was only to be a Miftrefs) as that the *Squire* fhould have done fomething for her above that extream Contempt which her Vices have fince brought upon her; whence moft who have heard even her own Pretences, have been uncharitable enough to conclude,

that

Of RIVELLA

so vile a Nature as hers could hardly ever have been otherwise; since extream Corruption does not all at once, but rather gradually seize upon such who have any Degree of Vertue in their Composition.

SOON after these Disappointments, *Rivella* receiv'd an anonymous Letter by the Penny-Post, to beg her to be next Day at twelve a Clock, all alone, in a Hackney-Coach, in the upper *Hyde-Park* near the Lodge: She ask'd *Cleander*'s Opinion; he assur'd her it was the Hand-writing of Lord *Crafty*, which was so particular that no body could be mistaken that had once seen it; he advised her to go to the Appointment, for that Lord had too much Respect for the fair Sex to do an Outrage to any Lady; accordingly she went and found that very Person alone in another Hackney-Coach; he alighted and came into hers: After the first Forms were over, he did not scruple to value himself upon defeating their well laid Design. He assur'd her they should never recover *Tim* again, and therefore advised her, since she understood so much of this Matter, to make up her Disappointments by indeavouring an Accommodation between the *Baron* and himself, to which end, his Lordship gave her Power to a certain Point, how to proceed.

THE *Baron* approv'd of the Project, he gave *Rivella* leave to treat with the Lord *Crafty*, with an Assurance of Two Thousand Pound for her self if they should, by her means, agree; and to shew his Lordship that *Cleander* and her self were *Trustworthy*, and very well deserved his Favour, she brought *Tim*'s only Brother, the next Heir in case *Tim* should have no Sons, to his Lordship; this poor young Man wanted Food, Raiment and Education, his Parts and Honesty much exceeded the Squires; he sold his Reversion to the *Baron* for an Annuity of an Hundred and Fifty Pounds a Year; and thought himself very happy to be able to secure a present Maintenance out of his imaginary future Hopes.

THIS was a Circumstance Lord *Crafty* could hardly forgive himself; looking upon *Tim* or his Lady to be fruitful Persons, tho' the Males all died, he never once consider'd his Brother might prove of Consequence: In short, his Lordship and *Rivella* often met, he did all that was in his Power to shake her Fidelity to the *Baron*; told her he laid Eighteen Thousand Pound a Year at her Feet, all his good Fortune had come by Ladies, but he had never found any of so great Ability as her self. He endeavour'd to make it her Interest to corrupt

rupt *Ofwald* to incline the *Baron* to eafier Terms of Accommodation; when he faw fhe was not to be fhaken, he confented to treat with the Lord *Meanwell* in Perfon, a Circumftance he had hitherto refufed her whenever fhe propofed it. They accordingly met where Lord *Crafty* extoll'd *Rivella* in fuch an artful Manner, that made the *Baron* fufpect fhe was in his Intereft, telling him he was fo well fatisfied in her Honour and Capacity, (for no Lawyer they had ever employ'd knew the Caufe fo well) that he would refer the whole Matter to the Decifion, and peremptorily offer'd to put it upon that very Iffue. The *Baron* at that Touch fhrank himfelf all in a Heap, like the fenfible Plant; he told *Ofwald*, that *that* very artful Lord had corrupted *Rivella*'s Truth, elfe how was it poffible he durft leave a Matter of fuch vaft Confequence to her Decifion: *Ofwald* had a better Opinion of her, and begg'd his Lordfhip, as a Proof that he would but feem to agree to *Crafty*'s Propofal, and then he would quickly find that what he faid was nothing but Pretence and Artifice: The *Baron* was not of his Opinion, believing himfelf wifer than all the World, and perhaps willing to fave the Money he had promifed *Rivella*, tho' it coft him much more the other way; he clapt up an hafty Agreement with *Crafty*, without any farther confulting *Ofwald* in the Matter, by which, out of old *Double*'s Eftate, he gave *That* Lord Threefcore and Twelve Thoufand Pound, and yet ftill remain'd liable to perform Conditions with *Tim*, when ever he fhould think fit to force him to it; but very much to his Mortification on one fide, and Joy on the other, he heard that *Tim* was kill'd with drinking, a juft and miferable Return for his Debauchery, Folly and Villany: If the *Baron* had known of his Death before the Agreement, it would have faved him feveral Thoufand Pounds; but fince the Agreement was made, he was very glad 'twas now become out of *Tim*'s Power to call his Lordfhip to an Account for that which he had made with him.

THUS my dear *D'Aumont*, continued Sir *Charles*, I have finifh'd the Secret Hiftory of that tedious Law Suit, which I juftly fear has likewife tir'd your Patience. My Bufinefs was to give you *Rivella*'s Hiftory on thofe Occafions that have to her Prejudice, made moft Noife in the World; fince fhe has writ for the *Tories*, the *Whigs* have heighten'd this Story, and too feverely reflected upon her for *Bella*'s Misfortunes, tho' they were all occafion'd by her own Vicioufnefs, Forwardnefs and Treachery, in which *Rivella* had not any Part. *Rivella* never faw nor applied her felf to the

The HISTORY

the *Baron* any more, nor conversed with *Oswald*. If that Lord ever made her an Acknowledgment, it was directed to miscarry, as coming thro' *Oswald*'s Hands, and she with Reason, reckons that Family to be much her Debtors: Poor *Cleander* was a great deal of Money out of Pocket, but he lov'd *Rivella* too well to reproach her with it.

DURING their mutual Intelligence and Friendship, *Calista*, after a long Disuse, came to visit *Rivella*; *Cleander* was then in the Room, they both look'd so amazed and confounded, that *Rivella* took the first Occasion to withdraw, to permit them an Opportunity to recover their Concern. If you remember *Chevalier*, *Calista* was the Lady who first ingaged *Rivella* to serve *Cleander*, tho' she excused her self upon being his Wife's Acquaintance, and not *Cleander*'s: When she had ended her Visit, *Rivella* would know what had occasion'd their mutual Confusion; he laugh'd and defended himself a long Time; at length, he confess'd *Calista* was the first Lady that had ever made him unfaithful to his Wife: Her Mother being in Misfortunes and indebted to him, she had offer'd her Daughter's Security, he took it, and moreover the Blessing of one Night's Lodging, which he never paid her back again.

Rivella

Rivella laugh'd in her Turn, becaufe *Califta* had given her felf Airs of not vifiting *Rivella*, now fhe was made the Town Talk by her fcandalous Intriegue with *Cleander*; *Rivella* defired him to give her the Bond, which he promifed and perform'd.

MUCH about that Time, *George* Prince of *Hefs Darmftad*, came the fecond Time into *England*; he had been *Vice-Roy* of *Catalonia*, towards the latter End of *Charles* the Third's Reign: The Inclination his Highnefs had of returning into *Spain*, his Adorations for the *Dowager*, his Relation being no Secret, made him keep up his Correfpondence with the *Catalans*; principally with the Inhabitants of *Barcelona*, who continually follicited him to Aid them with Forces, whereby they might be enabled to declare themfelves againft *Philip* of *Bourbon*, whom they unwillingly obey'd: The Prince of *Hefs* reprefented this to the Court of *England*, as a Matter of very great Importance; he produced feveral Letters from the chief Perfons of *Catalonia*: His Highnefs was recommended to a Merchant in the City, whom he pray'd to introduce him into the Acquaintance of fome of the moft ingenious Ladies of the *English* Nation; this Merchant was acquainted with a Gentlewoman that was newly fet up to fell *Milliner's ner*'s Ware to the Ladies and Gentlemen; she was well born, and incouraged by several Persons who laid out their Money with her in Consideration of her Misfortunes: The Merchant desir'd she would speak to the Lady *Rivella*, who was her Customer, and two Ladies more, to come one Evening to Cards at her House, where himself would introduce the Prince incog. His Highness understood nothing of *Loo*, which was the Game they play'd at; he could not speak a Word of *English*, nor the other Ladies a Word of *French*. They knew his Quality, tho' they were to take no notice of it, and thought to win his Money, which is all that most Ladies care for at Play: *Rivella* sat next the Prince, and for the Honour of the *English* Women would not let him be cheated, she assisted him in his Game, and in conjunction with his good Luck, order'd the Matter so well, that his Highness was the only Person who rose a Winner: From that Time he conceiv'd the greatest Esteem for *Rivella*, the Prince presented her with his Picture at length, and continued a Correspondence with her till the Day before his Death: *Cleander* did not believe there was any mixture of Love in it, because it was well known, the Prince had engaged his Heart in *Spain*, and his Person in *England*, by way of Amusement to a certain celebrated

ted Lady, who had made a great Figure in *Flanders*, and was more known by the Name of the *Electress* of *Bavaria*, than her own.

R I V E L L A tasted some Years the Pleasure of Retirement, in the Conversation of the Person beloved; but a tedious and an unhappy Law-Suit straitned *Cleander*'s Circumstances and put him under several Difficulties. In the mean time his Wife died; *Rivella* was complimented upon her Loss even by *Cleander* himself, for all the World thought he lov'd her so well as to marry her; she receiv'd his Address with such Confusion and Regret, that he knew not what to make of her Disorder, till at length bursting forth into Tears, she cry'd I am undone from this Moment! I have lost the only Person, who secured to me the Possession of your Heart! *Cleander* was struck with her Words, I came into the Room, and *Rivella* withdrew to hide her Concern: *Cleander* felt himself so wounded by what she had spoken, that I shall never forget it; he confess'd her to be the greatest Mistress of Nature that ever was born; she knew, he said, the hidden Springs and Defects of Human-kind; Self-love was indeed such an inherent Evil in all the World, that he was afraid *Rivella* had spoken something that look'd too like Truth; but what

what ever happened he fhould never be acquainted with a Woman of her Worth, neither could any thing but extream Neceffity, force him to abandon her Innocence and Tendernefs.

NOT long after *Cleander* was caft at Law, and condemn'd in a great Sum to be paid by the next Term; he conceal'd his Misfortunes from *Rivella*, but fhe learn'd them from other Perfons: One muft be a Woman of an exalted Soul to take the Part fhe did: The Troubles of the Mind caft her into a Fit of Sicknefs; *Cleander* guefs'd at the Caufe, and endeavour'd to reftore her at any Price, having affur'd her of it; fhe ask'd him if he would marry her; he immediately anfwer'd he would, tho' he were ruin'd by it; fhe told him that was a very hard Sentence, fhe could not confent to his ruin with half fo much eafe as to her own; then enquired if there was any Way to fave him? He explain'd to her his Circumftances, and the Propofals that had been made to him of courting a rich young Widow, but that he could not think of it: *Rivella* paus'd a long Time, at length pulling up her Spirits, and fixing her Refolution, fhe told him it fhould be fo; he fhould not be undone for her fake; fhe had receiv'd many Obligations from him, and he had fuffer'd feveral

Inconveniences on her Account; particularly in the Affair of Mr. *Timothy Double:* She was proud it was now in her Power to repay part of the Debt she ow'd; therefore she conjur'd him to make his Addresses to the Lady, for tho' he might be so far influenced by his Bride as afterwards to become ingrateful, she would much rather that should happen, than to see him Poor and Miserable, an Object of perpetual Reproach to her Heart and Eyes; for having preferr'd the Reparation of her own Honour, to the Preservation of his.

I SHOULD move you too far, Generous *D'Aumont,* in relating half that Tenderness and Reluctance, with which it was concluded they should part: I was the Confident between them; but tho' I had Esteem and Friendship for *Cleander,* there was something touch'd my Soul more nearly for *Rivella*'s Interest; therefore I would have disswaded her from that Romantick Bravery of Mind, by advising her to marry her Lover, who was so bright a Man, that he could never prove long unhappy, his own Capacity being sufficient to extricate him; but as she had never taken my Advice in any Thing, she did not begin now; there was a Pleasure she said in becoming Miserable, when it was to make a Person happy, by whom she had

Of RIVELLA.

had been so very much obliged, and so long and faithfully beloved!

CLEANDER's handsom Person immediately made Way to the Widow's Heart; it is not my Business to speak much of her, tho' the Theam be very ample; I have heard him say, that he might have succeeded to his Wish, if he could have had the Confidence to believe a Woman could have been won so quickly: Her Relations got notice of the Courtship, and represented the Disadvantage of the Match, which occasion'd Settlements and Security of her own Fortune to her own Use. *Cleander* trusted to the Power he hoped to gain over her Heart; thinking when once they were married, she might be brought to recede, but he was mistaken: *The woing lasted but a Month; with all the Obstacles her Friends could raise*, which perhaps was a Fortnight longer than the Date of her Passion afterwards. Fears and Jealousies ensu'd; they pass'd many uneasy Hours of Wedlock together. He teiz'd the Lady about Cards, and she him for *Rivella* who seldom saw him; for she led her Life mostly in the Country, and never appear'd in Publick after *Cleander*'s Marriage; which with four Years Uneasiness concluded in the Loss of his Senses, and in three more of his Life; whether the

Want of *Rivella*'s Converfation, which he had fo long been us'd to contributed, or the Uneafinefs of his Circumftances; for his Marriage had not anfwer'd the fancied End, or fomething elfe, which I am not willing to fay, where very much may be faid; tho' as *Rivella*'s Friend, I have no Reafon to fpare *Cleander*'s Lady, becaufe fhe always fpeaks of her with Language moft unfit for a Gentlewoman, and on all Occafions, has us'd her with the Spite and ill Nature of an enraged jealous Wife.

AFTER that Time, I know nothing memorable of *Rivella*, but that fhe feem'd to bury all Thoughts of Gallantry in *Cleander*'s Tomb; and unlefs fhe had her felf publifh'd fuch melting Scenes of Love, I fhould by her Regularity and good Behaviour have thought fhe had loft the Memory of that Paffion. I was in the Country when the Two firft Volumes of the *Atalantis* were Publifh'd, and did not know who was the Author, but came to Town juft as the Lord S——d had granted a Warrant againft the *Printer* and *Publifher*: I went as ufual, to wait upon *Rivella*, whom I found in one of her Heroick Strains; fhe faid fhe was glad I was come, to advife her in a Bufinefs of very great Importance; fhe had as yet confult-
ed

ed with but one Friend, whose Counsel had not pleas'd her; no more would mine, I thought, but did not interrupt her; in Conclusion she told me that her self was Author of the *Atalantis*, for which three innocent Persons were taken up and would be ruin'd with their Families; that she was resolv'd to surrender her self into the *Messenger*'s Hands, whom she heard had the Secretary of State's Warrant against her, so to discharge those honest People from their Imprisonment: I stared upon her and thought her directly mad; I began with railing at her Books; the barbarous Design of exposing People that never had done her any Injury; she answer'd me she was become *Misanthrope*, a perfect *Timon*, or *Man-Hater*; all the World was out of Humour with her, and she with all the World, more particularly a *Faction* who were busy to enslave their Sovereign, and overturn the Constitution; that she was proud of having more Courage than had any of our Sex, and of throwing the first Stone, which might give a Hint for other Persons of more Capacity to examine the Defects, and Vices of some Men who took a Delight to impose upon the World, by the Pretence of publick Good, whilst their true Design was only to gratify and advance themselves. As to exposing those who had

never

never injured her, she said she did no more by others, than others had done by her (*i.e.*) Tattle of Frailties; the Town had never shewn her any Indulgence, but on the contrary reported ten fold against her in Matters of which she was wholly Innocent; whereas she did but take up old Stories that all the World had long since reported, having ever been careful of glancing against such Persons who were truly vertuous, and who had not been very careless of their own Actions.

RIVELLA grew warm in her Defence, and obstinate in her Design of surrendring her self a Prisoner: I ask'd her how she would like going to *Newgate?* She answer'd me very well; since it was to discharge her Conscience; I told her all this sounded great, and was very Heroick; but there was a vast Difference between real and imaginary Sufferings: She had chose to declare her self of a Party most Supine, and forgetful of such who served them; that she would certainly be abandon'd by them, and left to perish and starve in Prison. The most severe Criticks upon *Tory* Writings, were *Tories* themselves, who never considering the Design or honest Intention of the Author, would examin the Performance only, and that too with as much Severity as they
would

would an Enemy's, and at the same Time value themselves upon their being impartial, tho' against their Friends: Then as to Gratitude or Generosity, the *Tories* did not come up to the *Whigs*, who never suffer'd any Man to want Incouragement and Rewards if he were never so dull, vicious or insignificant, provided he declar'd himself to be for them; whereas the *Tories* had no general Interest, and consequently no particular, each Person refusing to contribute towards the Benefit of the whole; and when it should come to pass (as certainly it would) that she perish'd thro' Want in a Goal, they would sooner condemn her Folly, than pitty her Sufferings; and cry, *she may take it for her Pains: Who bid her write? What good did she do? Could not she sit quiet as well as her Neighbours, and not meddle her self about what did not concern her?*

RIVELLA was startled at these Truths, and ask'd me, What then would I have her do? I answer'd that I was still at her Service, as well as my Fortune: I would wait upon her out of *England*, and then find some Means to get her safe into *France*, where the Queen, that was once to have been her Mistress, would doubtless take her into her own Protection; she said the Project was a vain one,

one, that Lady being the greateſt Bigot in Nature to the *Roman* Church, and ſhe was, and ever would be, a *Proteſtant*, a Name ſufficient to deſtroy the greateſt Merit in that Court. I told her I would carry her into *Switzerland*, or any Country that was but a Place of Safety, and leave her there if ſhe commanded me; ſhe ask'd me in a haſty Manner, as if ſhe demanded Pardon for heſitating upon the Point, what then would become of the poor *Printer*, and thoſe two other Perſons concern'd, the *Publiſhers*, who with their Families all would be undone by her Flight? That the Miſery I had threaten'd her with, was a leſs Evil than doing a diſhonourable Thing: I ask'd her if ſhe had promis'd thoſe Perſons to be anſwerable for the Event? She ſaid no, ſhe had only given them leave to ſay, if they were queſtion'd, *they had receiv'd the Copy from her Hand!* I us'd ſeveral Arguments to ſatisfy her Conſcience that ſhe was under no farther Obligation, eſpecially ſince the Profit had been theirs; ſhe anſwer'd it might be ſo, but ſhe could not bear to live and reproach her ſelf with the Miſery that might happen to thoſe unfortunate People: Finding her obſtinate, I left her with an angry Threat, of never beholding her in that wretched State, into which ſhe was going to plunge her ſelf.

Of RIVELLA

RIVELLA remain'd immovable in a Point which she thought her Duty, and accordingly surrender'd her self, and was examin'd in the Secretary's Office: They us'd several Arguments to make her discover who were the Persons concern'd with her in writing her Books; or at least from whom she had receiv'd Information of some special Facts, which they thought were above her own Intelligence: Her Defence was with much Humility and Sorrow, for having offended, at the same Time denying that any Persons were concern'd with her, or that she had a farther Design than writing for her own Amusement and Diversion in the Country; without intending particular Reflections or Characters: When this was not believ'd, and the contrary urg'd very home to her by several Circumstances and Likenesses; she said then it must be *Inspiration*, because knowing her own Innocence she could acount for it no other Way: The Secretary reply'd upon her, that *Inspiration* us'd to be upon a good Account, and her Writings were stark naught; she told him, with an Air full of Penitence, that might be true, but it was as true, that there were evil Angels as well as good; so that nevertheless what she had wrote might still be by *Inspiration*.

NOT to detain you longer, dear attentive *D'Aumont*, the gathering Clouds beginning to bring Night upon us, this poor Lady was close shut up in the *Messenger*'s Hands from seeing or speaking to any Person, without being allow'd Pen, Ink and Paper; where she was most tyranically and barbarously insulted by the Fellow and his Wife who had her in keeping, tho' doubtless without the Knowledge of their Superiors; for when *Rivella* was examin'd, they ask'd her if she was civilly us'd? She thought it below her to complain of such little People, who when they stretch'd Authority a little too far, thought perhaps that they serv'd the Intention and Resentments, tho' not the Commands of their Masters; and accordingly chose to be inhuman, rather than just and civil.

RIVELLA's Council sued out her *Habeas Corpus* at the *Queen*'s *Bench-Bar* in *Westminster* Hall; and she was admitted to Bail. Whether the Persons in Power were ashamed to bring a Woman to her Trial for writing a few amorous Trifles purely for her own Amusement, or that our Laws were defective, as most Persons conceiv'd, because she had serv'd her self with Romantick Names, and a feign'd Scene of Action? But after several

veral Times expoſing her in Perſon to walk croſs the Court before the Bench of Judges, with her three Attendants, the *Printer* and both the *Publiſhers*; the *Attorny General* at the End of three or four Terms dropt the Proſecution, tho' not without a very great Expence to the Defendants, who were however glad to compound with their Purſes for their heinious Offence, and the notorious Indiſcretion of which they had been guilty.

THERE happen'd not long after a total Change in the Miniſtry, the Perſons whom *Rivella* had diſoblig'd being removed, and conſequently her Fears diſſipated; upon which that native Gaiety and good Humour ſo ſparkling and conſpicuous in her, return'd; I had the hardeſt Part to act, becauſe I could not eaſily forego her Friendſhip and Acquaintance, yet knew not very well how to pretend to the Continuance of either, conſidering what I had ſaid to her upon our laſt Seperation the Night before her Impriſonment: Finding I did not return to wiſh her Joy with the reſt of her Friends upon her Inlargement, ſhe did me the Favour to write to me, aſſuring me that ſhe very well diſtinguiſh'd that which a Friend out of the Greatneſs of his Friendſhip did adviſe, and what a Man of Honour

nour could be suppos'd to endure, by giving Advice wherein his Friend or himself must suffer, and that since I had so generously endeavour'd her Safety at the expence of my own Character, she would always look upon me as a Person whom nothing could taint but my Friendship for her. I was asham'd of the Delicacy of her Argument, by which since I was prov'd guilty, tho' the Motives were never so prevalent, still my Honour was found defective, how perfect soever my Friendship might appear.

RIVELLA had always the better of me at this Argument, and when she would insult me, never fail'd to serve her self with that false one, *Success*, in return, I brought her to be asham'd of her Writings, saving that Part by which she pretended to serve her Country, and the ancient Constitution; (there she is a perfect *Bigot* from a long untainted Descent of Loyal Ancestors, and consequently immoveable) but when I would argue with her the Folly of a Woman's disobliging any one Party, by a Pen equally qualified to divert all, she agreed my Reflection was just, and promis'd not to repeat her Fault, provided the World would have the Goodness to forget those she had already committed, and that henceforward

forward her Business should be to write of Pleasure and Entertainment only, wherein *Party* should no longer mingle; but that the *Whigs* were so unforgiving they would not advance one Step towards a *Coalition* with any Muse that had once been so indiscreet to declare against them: She now agrees with me, that Politicks is not the Business of a Woman, especially of one that can so well delight and entertain her Readers with more gentle pleasing Theams, and has accordingly set her self again to write a Tragedy for the Stage. If you stay in *England*, dear *Chevalier*, till next Winter, we may hope to entertain you from thence, with what ever *Rivella* is capable of performing in the *Dramatick* Art.

BUT has she still a Taste for Love, interrupted young Monsieur *D'Aumont*? Doubtless, answer'd Sir *Charles*, or whence is it that she daily writes of him with such Fire and Force? But whether she does Love, is a Question? I often hear her Express a Jealousy of appearing fond at her Time of Day, and full of Rallery against those Ladies, who sue when they are no longer sued unto. She converses now with our Sex in a Manner that is very delicate, sensible, and agreeable; which is to say, knowing her self to be no longer Young, she does not seem to expect the Praise and
Flat-

Flattery that attend the Youthful: The greatest Genius's of the Age, give her daily Proofs of their Esteem and Friendship; only one excepted, who yet I find was more in her Favour than any other of the Wits pretend to have been, since he in Print has very lately told the World, 'twas his own Fault he was not Happy, for which Omission he has publickly and gravely ask'd her Pardon. Whether this Proceeding was so *Chevalier* as is ought, I will no more determine against him, than believe him against her; but since the charitable Custom of the World gives the Lie to that Person, whosoever he be, that boasts of having receiv'd a Lady's Favour, because it is an Action unworthy of Credit, and of a Man of Honour; may not he by the same Rule be disbeliev'd, who says he might and would not receive Favours; especially from a Sweet, Clean, Witty, Friendly, Serviceable and young Woman, as *Rivella* was, when this Gentleman pretends to have been *Cruel*; considering that in the Choice of his other Amours, he has given no such Proof of his Delicacy, or the Niceness of his Taste? But what shall we say, the Prejudice of *Party* runs so high in *England*, that the best natured Persons, and those of the greatest Integrity, scruple not to say False and Malicious Things of those who differ from them in Principles, in any Case

but

Of RIVELLA.

but Love; Scandal between *Whig* and *Tory*, goes for nothing; but who is there besides my self, that thinks it an impossible Thing a *Tory* Lady should prove frail, especially when a Person (tho' never so much a *Whig*) reports her to be so, upon his own Knowledge.

THUS generous *D'Aumont*, I have endeavour'd to obey your Commands, in giving you that part of *Rivella*'s History, which has made the most Noise against her; I confess, had I shown only the bright Part of her Adventures; I might have Entertain'd you much more agreeably, but that requires much longer Time; together with the Songs, Letters and Adorations, innumerable from those who never could be Happy. Then to have rais'd your Passions in her Favour; I should have brought you to her Table well furnish'd and well serv'd; have shown you her sparkling Wit and easy Gaiety, when at Meat with Persons of Conversation and Humour: From thence carried you (in the Heat of Summer after Dinner) within the Nymphs Alcove, to a Bed nicely sheeted and strow'd with *Roses*, *Jessamins* or *Orange-Flowers*, suited to the variety of the Season; her Pillows neatly trim'd with Lace or Muslin, stuck round with *Junquils*, or other natural Garden Sweets, for she uses no Perfumes,

and

and there have given you leave to fancy your felf the happy Man, with whom fhe chofe to repofe her felf, during the Heat of the Day, in a State of Sweetnefs and Tranquility: From thence conducted you towards the cool of the Evening, either upon the *Water*, or to the *Park* for Air, with a Converfation always new, and which never cloys; *Allon*'s let us go my dear *Lovemore*, interrupted young *D'Aumont*, let us not lofe a Moment before we are acquainted with the only Perfon of her Sex that knows how to *Live*, and of whom we may fay, in relation to Love, fince fhe has fo peculiar a Genius for, and has made fuch noble Difcoveries in that Paffion, that it would have been a *Fault in her, not to have been Faulty.*

FINIS.

THE LIBRARY
ST. MARY'S COLLEGE OF MARYLAND
ST. MARY'S CITY, MARYLAND 20686

DATE DUE			
	PA LIB RTD	SEP 2 0 2007	